WallStreet.com

WallStreet.com

Fat Cat Investing
at the Click of a Mouse

· · · · ·

How Andy Klein and
the Internet Can Give Everyone
a Seat on the Exchange

Andrew D. Klein

HENRY HOLT AND COMPANY · NEW YORK

Henry Holt and Company, Inc.
Publishers since 1866
115 West 18th Street
New York, New York 10011

Henry Holt® is a registered trademark of
Henry Holt and Company, Inc.

Published in Canada by Fitzhenry & Whiteside Ltd.,
195 Allstate Parkway, Markham, Ontario L3R 4T8.

Library of Congress Cataloging-in-Publication Data
Klein, Andrew D.
WallStreet.com: fat cat investing at the click of a mouse;
how Andy Klein and the Internet can give everyone a seat on
the exchange / Andrew D. Klein.
p.   cm.
Includes index.
ISBN 0-8050-5758-7 (alk. paper)
1. Electronic trading of securities. 2. Going public (Securities)
I. Title.
HG4515.95.K55 1998   97-32601
332. 64'0285—dc21   CIP

Henry Holt books are available for special promotions
and premiums. For details contact: Director, Special Markets.

First Holt Edition 1998

Designed by Victoria Hartman

Printed in the United States of America
All first editions are printed on acid-free paper. ∞
1   3   5   7   9   10   8   6   4   2

Contents

WallStreet.com

Introduction
My Digital Dream

Picture a plush private dining room, high above Manhattan. Polished walnut paneling on the walls and an Aubusson carpet on the floor mute the rough edges of conversation from the thirty power-suited businesspeople gathered in the room. Outside the floor-to-ceiling windows, the world's most famous skyline glitters like diamonds. Inside, discreet waiters continually refill crystal goblets with wine priced at $400 a bottle. The cuisine is *nouvelle américaine*, the china antique Limoges. Everything within reach—everything in sight—is the top of the line, the best you can get.

The occasion is an IPO (Initial Public Offering) closing dinner, one of the investment world's most cherished rituals. The company hosting the dinner has made an IPO of its stock; it has "gone public," selling shares on the open market for the first time. The dinner celebrates that fact, and it brings together, for the last time, the bankers and investors and lawyers who made it happen.

But the dinner is something else as well. It is a meeting of a very private, very exclusive club. The members of this club have in common that they are the guaranteed winners in the IPO process. When American companies raise capital by selling shares on the stock market, these people cannot lose.

The institutions and very wealthy individuals who have bought the company's first stock issue cannot lose because the investment bankers got them a bargain-basement price. All they have to do is hold on to the stock until the public starts to bid up the price, then flip their shares to smaller investors and pocket the profit.

The investment bankers cannot lose because they are making 7 percent on the sale of the issue. No wonder they have traveled far and wide to hold meetings, to stage presentations, to arrange lavishly persuasive lunches and dinners with potential investors. No wonder they have urged a wide network of brokers to promote this stock to retail investors and smaller institutions. The more the issue raises, the bigger their success.

The lawyers cannot lose because lawyers almost never do. For their hard work late at night and on weekends—regiments of lawyers poring over every detail of the stock offering prospectus—they have billed hundreds of thousands of dollars.

The company cannot lose because its coffers are now awash with money. It has raised capital—perhaps, since the offering price was so low, not quite as much as management would have liked, but enough to carry out plans.

Who loses in the IPO process? With all these guaranteed winners taking the choicest morsels, who gets the pickings that are left?

You do.

You, the retail investor. The millions of American shareholders who tend to hold on to the stocks you buy, thus providing the company its base of financial support. You're virtually shut out of the initial part of an Initial Public Offering. You're almost always cut off from that alluring offering price. That goes to the big guys—the institutions, the funds, the super-millionaires. After they have bought up the bulk of the issue, it's your turn. But not until then. And not without the big guys raking in a hefty profit.

This is the dirty little secret of American investing: while the institutional investors and mega-wealthy individuals are welcomed through the front door and offered first pick at the goods—and a discount price—retail investors are asked to go around to the back door, wait for the leftovers, and pay through the nose.

There's another side to this secret. The fact is, the company issuing the stock has most likely been muscled into undervaluing its stock, setting a lower offering price than it could have gotten in a truly competitive process. That's because the leverage is with the investment banks and the big institutional buyers. The conventional wisdom is that they are the only game in town. So when they exert pressure on the company issuing the stock, the company invariably knuckles under. Then the investment bankers go to work. Networks of retail brokers promote the stock. The public starts buying, and the stock price shoots up from its artificially low offering price.

Then there is the king's ransom the company has to pay just to get its stock to market: fees for that army of lawyers billing hundreds of dollars an hour; the substantial costs to print, package, and distribute the prospectus; plus travel and accommodations for the investment bankers shopping the deal around the country—maybe around the world—delivering glossy presentations, staying in first-class hotels, wining and dining prospective institutional investors over expense-account lunches.

Not to mention the closing dinner. In the time it's taken to describe why it's being held, the participants have finished a *bombe aux trois chocolats*, washed down by a Château d'Yquem sauterne, and have moved on to the final course of aged cheese and fresh fruit, accompanied by vintage port and fine cognacs. Like the IPO process itself, the closing dinner is costly for the hosts, delicious and highly rewarding for the guests, and limited to members only.

How do I know? How is it I'm so familiar with these clever mysteries of American capital formation? That's easy: I've been there.

As a securities lawyer at Cravath, Swaine & Moore, one of Wall Street's legendary firms, I've been in the room when these dirty little secrets were being spun. I've helped prep the investment bankers and company executives for their high-priced road show of presentations to investors, sent limousines to pick up important papers, ordered sumptuous meals when I was working late on a prospectus, drunk champagne at the closing dinner—all at the expense of the company issuing the stock. Ultimately, of course, that expense is borne by the shareholders—mostly the retail investors—who buy and keep the stock that is issued.

I've seen the system at work. I've seen it close enough to get a good look at the hidden infrastructure rigged to the benefit of a privileged few at the old-boy network that exacts outrageous tolls on new companies seeking capital, at the squandering of shareholder money on promotions and perks, at a stock exchange system that enriches layers of middlemen who form a wall between companies and the ordinary people who would like to invest in them.

I've been one of those middlemen. A junior member of the club. An operative in the system who helped make it work. But now, with a little help from the Internet, I'm hoping to change the system forever.

How? I have created a financial marketplace on the World Wide Web, a company known as Wit Capital Corporation, that uses technology to give ordinary investors access to products and services that historically have been available only to large institutions and very, very wealthy individuals. Wit Capital is a new breed of investment bank that distributes new-issue securities. It is a registered broker-dealer that executes stock trades at rates that are a small fraction of traditional brokers' commissions, as well as a digital stock market that will electronically, directly match buy and sell orders and execute them. It's also something more than the sum of those parts; it's a community of on-line investors—an open, egalitarian financial marketplace.

As an investment bank, Wit Capital provides individual investors opportunities to invest in IPOs at the offering price. It also gives investors, for the first time ever, a meaningful chance to invest in growth companies that are in the early stages of development. Today, only venture capital institutions, large corporate investors, and millionaire "angel" investors have that opportunity.

It means that the price of admission to an IPO is access to a computer, an Internet service provider, a telephone, and a few clicks of the keyboard. You'll just log on, go to http://www.witcapital.com on the World Wide Web, check what's new in stock offerings, read—or watch and listen to—a revolutionary kind of prospectus, gain access to the same information once given only to the big institutional buyers, decide what you want to do, then execute your decision.

The Internet levels the playing field, and both stock issuers and stock buyers reap the benefits. Instead of a bunch of middlemen playing their roles and in turn taking their splits, all parties can deal with one another immediately, simply, and directly. Cheaply, too. No more exaggerated investment banking fees. No more excessive costs of printing and distributing prospectuses, either. Instead of taking the sales pitch on the road to woo giant hedge-fund managers, millions of regular investors can easily and cheaply find the sales pitch on the Web. All of that reduces the cost of raising capital, giving more companies access to the capital-raising process and offering more investors a shot at higher profits that can come with investment in companies before the public-offering stage. That's good for everybody.

Meanwhile, by automating the matching of buy and sell orders, electronic trading will deliver the first truly open market. On the Web, you won't be captive to specialists or market-makers and their expensive spreads. Best price will be determined directly between buyer and seller. It's the free market as it was meant to be, with supply and demand setting the terms of a transaction.

Wit Capital, in short, aims to democratize our capital markets. In doing so, it will transform the markets—both here in the United States and, potentially, throughout the world.

This book is the story of that transformation. It tells you everything your broker knows full well but will never in a million years tell you: about the almost malicious way capital formation works today, about how Wall Street as an institution has no interest in treating individual investors, about how the members of the private and exclusive Wall Street club keep it private and exclusive.

This book *will* tell you. It will tell why the club members are entirely happy with the way Wall Street works today. After all, if the system were rigged in your favor, wouldn't you be happy with it? Wouldn't you resist changing it? This book will tell you why the present, entrenched system of capital formation in this country needs to have a fire lit under it—for the benefit of the economy at large and all the players in the economy. And it explains how Wit Capital is fueling that fire—right at the door to the club.

This book is also my story. It tells how I went from being an apprentice of the present system, to an entrepreneur trying to use the system to actually raise capital, to a revolutionary working to change that system fundamentally.

Finally, this book is the story of what I think the enlightenment can mean—not just for me but for millions of individual investors and entrepreneurs around the world. Wit Capital, along with other players in the electronic financial marketplace, is challenging some of the fundamental structures and practices of Wall Street. In doing so, we are also challenging Wall Street's hegemony and Wall Street's complacency. I believe the challenge can be good for Wall Street, serving as a goad to the investment establishment to change those structures and practices for the better.

Wit Capital will open the market to more companies and more investors, and it will create more opportunities for both. That's my digital dream. This book tells how I'm trying to make the dream come true.

1.

One Learning Experience after Another

It all started with beer.

Cold beer on a hot day at the ballpark. Beer in a bottle, no glass, served in a neon-lit bar. The beaded keg of beer at the family picnic on the Fourth of July. Beer and potato chips and overstuffed sandwiches in front of the television set during football season. During my teenage years, on these and other occasions, I drank my share, paying little attention to just what it was I was drinking.

That changed in 1980. I was an undergraduate at Brandeis at the time—and a varsity soccer player—when a chance encounter in a Burger King in Boston led me into a whole new world of barley, malt, and hops. Also dining in Burger King that night was a touring English soccer club coach named Les Thwates, who claimed to be, among other things, a talent scout for West Ham United, one of Britain's most famous professional teams. Les was impressed with the enthusiasm my buddies and I displayed for his national sport, so much so that, within minutes, he extended a remarkable offer: he invited three of us to come to London to train with West Ham. It was an extraordinary opportunity. Football, association football as it is officially called, is *the* spectator sport of Britain as of most countries on earth, and West Ham United, if not a championship team, consistently brought respectable credit to its maroon and baby blue colors. Excited and flattered, we decided to seize the opportunity. We took leaves of absence from college, borrowed money, and on a cold January day set off for East London to pursue glory as professional soccer players under the tutelage of Mr. Ed Bailey, coach of West Ham United.

But Mr. Ed Bailey, as it turned out, was not exactly expecting us. Mr. Bailey had never heard of Les Thwates. Nor was he terribly interested in allowing American college kids to train with his team. "Do ya Yankees even play football?" he asked.

We insisted we did. We tried charm and flattery: Nothing would give us greater pleasure than training with the mighty Hammers, as the West Ham players are called. We tried guilt: We had left school, spent money, invested in a future with West Ham. The coach finally relented. He agreed to let us practice with the team for six months.

The next day, we found a flat, rented beds, and moved in. The day after that, I went looking for some sort of employment so I could pay my rent. The employment I found in that spring of 1980—modestly gainful but entirely illegal, as I did not have a work visa—was as bartender in the Pimlico Tram, a neighborhood pub a few blocks from London's Victoria Station. There, just before my twentieth birthday, I had my first taste of real English ale. Then my first English bitter. My first authentic porter. And eventually, my first pint of Irish stout. It was the beginning of an astonishing six months.

By day, I kicked, dribbled, headed, and ran around Upton Park, West Ham's home field, practicing my game. By night, I drew down pints, served drinks, and watched the locals socialize.

The time flew by. West Ham had a miracle season, beating Arsenal in the final of the FA Cup—the Football Association championship that is akin to the Super Bowl. My playing skills—and those of my two compatriots—improved substantially, but so did our sense of realism. After six months with the pros, it was clear there was no way we were ever going to make it. So when the season's final whistle blew in May, we headed to the mainland of Europe, where we spent the summer trying to meet girls. There were the rendezvous in sidewalk cafés in Paris and Amsterdam. There were parties under the stars on the beaches of Mykonos and Santoríni. And everywhere, in every country and every port of call, there was more beer. From the North Sea to the Mediterranean, the array of beers was staggering— a real education for an American for whom, only a short time ago, beer had meant nothing more than a cold Bud, the taste and texture of which were not even an issue.

Back at Brandeis, I began to focus on a different kind of education. I had decided to go to law school, for which a good academic record demonstrating seriousness of purpose would be required. I made the grades and did well on the entrance exams, and in the fall of 1983 I entered Harvard Law School.

It has been said that getting into Harvard is tougher and more rewarding than the education itself. That was certainly my experience. In the dreaded first year of law school, I studied quite hard—at least for about three weeks at the end of the first semester and for perhaps another six at the end of the academic year. During my second and third years, however, I studied very little. In fact, I barely went to class.

This was not out of indifference to the subject matter. As an undergraduate, my thesis had explored the moral rationale of affirmative action, and I remained intensely curious about how society used legal and governmental systems to resolve competition among various points of view, economic interests, and conceptions of fairness or justice. Nor did I lack respect for the law school's professors, who were uniformly dedicated teachers as well as great scholars.

Still, I was troubled by what I saw as a fundamental flaw in the day-to-day process of legal education.

As future lawyers, we were taught how to navigate the legal landscape, how to listen like lawyers and talk like lawyers, and how laws are made—no simple matter in a legal system that includes federal and state laws, constitutional laws, statutory laws, administrative laws, and laws made by judges.

Harvard's method of teaching all this is the famed case system, in which students are required to read lots of court cases—perhaps hundreds of pages in preparation for a single lesson on a single topic of law—and then sit through class sessions in which professors grill individual students in an intellectual fencing match that is supposed to resemble Socratic dialogue. What are the facts of the case? What did the lawyers argue? What did the judge rule? What was the court's stated rationale? Books have been written about Harvard Law's class sessions, and, of course, a popular movie, *The Paper Chase*, illustrated it all too well.

The truth is, however, that the teacher-student exchanges, while yielding the occasional laugh and the odd burst of insight, often seemed unreasonably competitive, painfully slow moving, and just plain boring. When it became clear that much of what went on in class could be captured from published outlines available in the local bookstore, a lot of us just stopped going to class.

Instead, we slept late. Read newspapers under shade trees in Harvard yard. Went running. Played basketball. Hung out with friends. And of course, drank beer. Increasingly, we gave thought to what we were going to do when graduation put an end to this idyll and forced us into the real world of work.

Not that we had to worry about finding jobs. If the corporate world was where we wanted to be, Harvard Law School was an automatic entry pass and meal ticket. And in the go-go eighties, when corporate America was merging and acquiring and issuing stocks and junk bonds like mad, the law firms and investment banks seemed to have an insatiable appetite for graduates of the top law schools.

To get the young hotshots, the law firms and investment banks orchestrated aggressive, competitive recruiting campaigns, right on the campuses of Harvard and other high-powered law schools. Before the first year's first semester had ended, hundreds of law firms had sent representatives to Cambridge to recruit for summer jobs promising $1,300 a week in salary. (This was in the eighties, mind you; who knows what they're offering today.) All you had to do was pick a firm, throw on decent clothes, and show up on campus to snag a twenty-minute interview. By the time you pedaled back home to change clothes again, you could expect a friendly message on the answering machine inviting you to fly out for a visit, meet the partners, go to lunch.

My first summer job, after my first year at law school, was at the New York branch of a large Richmond-based firm, Hunton & Williams. In the second summer, I split the fifteen weeks of the vacation and took two jobs. Given how little effort I was putting out during the school year, and with the opportunity cost pegged at $1,300 a week, I managed to live without taking "time off" for a rest at the beach. Instead, I spent eight weeks at Simpson, Thacher & Bartlett in New York and seven more at McCutchen, Doyle in San Francisco.

The summer stints at these law firms were more about being courted than about being put to work. To some extent, of course, the firms saw the summers as a chance to look over the crop of students, then select the most outstanding or promising. But it was also true that they wanted the students to enjoy the experience—so that you would at best return as a full-time employee, at least speak highly of the firm to other potential recruits back at law school.

So they treated us like royalty, until it was hard not to feel like a young prince being pursued by the father of every beautiful princess in the kingdom.

In addition to the meetings with important clients, lunches with the brass, power breakfasts with senior partners, and special seminars arranged solely for us, no expense was spared to ensure that we got the message: that a few years of toil for the firm would lead inevitably to a lifetime of financial rewards and security.

And just to be certain, we were given very tangible demonstrations of just what the rewards could be: Weekends at the vacation estates of wealthy partners. A clambake at a beachfront mansion in East Hampton, Long Island. A barbecue at a private vineyard in Sonoma County. Golf outings at exclusive country clubs. Night games at the ballpark—in box seats behind third base.

Both firms in my second summer had an open lunch policy: go to any restaurant of your choice, every day, for as long a lunch as you like, without regard to cost, so long as you invite at least one permanent associate to go along. Each and every day.

The prize for pampering, however, surely went to Simpson

Thacher, which took the free money culture to the greatest extreme. In addition to the lunches, luxury weekends, and scheduled group outings to Yankee Stadium, each summer recruit was entitled to five "dream nights" on the town in New York City. We were allowed three guests for each of the five nights, but that limit on the number of people was about the only restriction imposed. All expenses were paid for the finest restaurants, for tickets to the hottest shows in town, for entrée into the trendiest clubs, for the skybox at Madison Square Garden, for the taxis or limos to get us where we were going, and for the generous tips we were encouraged to distribute.

One recruit—from the year before me—was legendary for one of his dream nights: a dinner in the Hamptons. He blithely hired a helicopter to fly himself and his three guests there and back. In this case, the firm did blink. Some controls were established after the incident, but some partners still may have considered it good training for fraternizing with rich clients. One could argue that it was simply the bait required to lure talented prey into the firm's web—instilling in us the idea that the glamour of champagne living more than repaid the hard reality of never-ending labor.

I think it was all of that and more. It seemed to me there was an underlying value at work, the sense that all this lavish spending conferred importance, that it lent an aura of power both to the law firms dispensing the cash and to the law-school grinds enjoying the perks. Did this money bestow authority? Would more money mean more authority?

Perhaps I had misgivings even then about large corporate law firms and the culture of big money that flourished within and around them. In any event, I decided to put off any decision about my future for at least another year. Instead, to buy time and give myself a perch from which to survey the world of law, I accepted a one-year postgraduate position as law clerk to Judge Irving R. Kaufman, at seventy-eight the chief judge of the United States Court of Appeals for the Second Circuit.

As perches go, this one should have been great. After the U.S.

Supreme Court, the federal appellate courts are the most powerful in the land. And because New York is a world financial and business center, the Second Circuit, which has jurisdiction there, is one of the most influential in the country. As chief judge, Kaufman wielded considerable power, controlling the court's calendar and influencing the roster of other judges and of the lawyers who appeared before him.

Kaufman's major claim to fame, however, stemmed from a case he had presided over as a young judge: the espionage charge against Julius and Ethel Rosenberg. Kaufman not only sentenced the pair to death, a sentence carried out in October 1954, but he also made a number of dubious judicial decisions at the time that facilitated the FBI's futile efforts to coerce the Rosenbergs into a confession. For the rest of his life, Kaufman would try in vain to downplay his association with that famous—perhaps notorious—case, to gain some distinction other than that of "the judge who sentenced the Rosenbergs."

By my third day as his law clerk, I decided the judge was an absolute lunatic. Obsessed by the Rosenberg case and embittered by his inevitable association with it, Kaufman had become a monumentally nasty man, rabidly short-tempered with everyone who had to deal with him: fellow judges, lawyers, secretaries, and, above all, law clerks.

At one point, in fact, all three of his law clerks, myself included, resigned en masse, flatly refusing to take any more of Kaufman's ranting and raving. After the judge apologized and turned on his not inconsiderable charm, I agreed to finish my one-year commitment. To his credit, Kaufman did reform his behavior, at least where I was concerned.

And there was value to be gained from working for him. First, since Kaufman refused to read the copious briefs submitted by counsel on cases ranging from complex securities litigation to criminal appeals, we law clerks had to. What's more, Kaufman then made us summarize each case in a three-page bench memo, reduce that to a single-page summary, then use a single file card to crystallize the main issue of the case and suggest two or three questions he should ask from the bench. One result was that I learned a great deal about a great variety of legal issues. Forced to home in on the core of each issue, I also learned how to cut to the heart of a case and extract its essence. It was good training in legal complexities and in how to think and speak precisely, as well as an object lesson in how not to be a judge. Another result, of course, was that Kaufman's irresponsible rejection of the hard work of the cases gave the law clerks the power to shape his vote on just about every matter. It was reprehensible on Kaufman's part, heady stuff for us twenty-something neophytes.

Short of impeachment, there's not much you can do about a judge like Kaufman. In this case, however, politics intervened. The Reagan administration was trying hard to fill the federal courts with judges who shared their ideological perspective on such vexing social issues as abortion and school prayer. Kaufman, for all his sins, was a generally liberal jurist who had held the line on such issues for years—and in a particularly influential court; that's why Reagan and his then-attorney general, Ed Meese, really wanted Kaufman's seat.

What Kaufman really wanted, of course, was a cleansing of his reputation that would restore balance to his legacy as a learned and important jurist. The attorney general offered Kaufman a deal: the President's Medal of Freedom, highest civilian award the U.S. government bestows, if Kaufman would resign his seat on the court.

Kaufman dealt. He gave up his seat to a young Republican appointed by Reagan, and Reagan gave Kaufman a Medal of Freedom.

I in turn gave up my sublet, took the bar exam, and fled to Europe. I wanted one last burst of travel before I looked for a new apartment, bought some suits and ties, and began what I had by now accepted as inevitable: my career as a corporate lawyer.

2.

Confessions of an Unhappy Lawyer

In the mid-1980s, when I was just beginning my education in beer—not to mention in law, lunatics, and how to spend corporate expense account money—the beverage of choice in the world I was preparing to enter was wine. Fine wine. It was a dizzying time for anyone involved with any aspect of Wall Street—a wild party with a groaning board of riches. Not-yet-thirty-year-olds bought BMWs with cash, dressed in Armani suits, shuttled between lavish Manhattan apartments and spacious weekend country homes. For investment bankers, money managers, traders, brokers, and, of course, for the lawyers who worked with all of them, the world was anything *but* beer. How do you celebrate stock market killings that made some people millionaires overnight—and made a few people billionaires overnight? With sparkling champagne-vintage Cristal.

I reported for duty the last week of November 1987, at the downtown offices of Cravath, Swaine & Moore, the venerable Wall Street partnership with roots dating back nearly two hundred years. Why Cravath? Simpson Thacher had extended a competitive offer, and there was any number of other firms willing to employ me.

My year with Judge Kaufman, however, had given me time to digest the early experiences of various law-school classmates sprinkled at the top corporate law firms. From that perspective, something about Cravath made it stand out. At all the other firms, young lawyers were assigned to one particular area of practice—either mergers and acquisitions, or underwriting, or banking. The idea was that they would quickly gain expertise in that area and become specialists. Cravath, by contrast, insisted that its new hires become generalists before settling down to one particular practice. From first-year rookies right up to eighth-year veterans on the verge of partnership, every associate rotated from one practice to another. That meant that associates were constantly confronting new challenges and entering unknown areas until, it was believed, they gained wide knowledge and important survival skills.

Whether I was lured by the firm's distinguished reputation as an incomparable school of future legal stars or simply that I could not imagine sticking with one practice, I do not know. But with its top-notch reputation and blue-chip client list, Cravath seemed a good place to start.

I was right. Despite all the horror stories about cold and calculating corporate law firms, just about everybody I met at Cravath was kind, considerate, and intelligent. Many became my friends. Together, we had a lot of fun.

Cravath's renowned sink-or-swim policy was rigorous, demanding, and invaluable. Young lawyers were expected to jump right into extremely complex matters, master the details, respond creatively and decisively, and contribute results. Those who survived this crash course in law, management, human relations, and life as it's really lived could soon handle anything. This education did not come cheap—we paid dearly in late nights, canceled weekends, delayed vacations, and sometimes unrelenting pressure—but the opportunity to learn from the best and to assume responsibility early on was priceless.

I spent my first twelve months shadowing senior partner Bob Rosenman, renowned as one of the nation's top securities lawyers. I watched him at the drafting sessions with bankers and lawyers poring over the details of a prospectus. I carried his bags across country while he did due diligence on companies preparing to go public. And I listened as he led long and sometimes tense negotiations with federal regulators scrutinizing new types of securities our investment banking clients were preparing to issue.

After Rosenman, I worked in a group dealing in hostile mergers and acquisitions. By day I sat in conference rooms as my senior colleagues developed strategies, analyzed structures, crafted—or tried to overcome—complex defenses such as poison pills, crown jewel lock-ups, and golden parachutes. By night, we young associates were expected to stay up late checking disclosure documents, compiling copious federal filing packages, researching every possible peripheral legal issue. It was grueling work, with high stakes, requiring mind-numbing attention to every detail. Still, I was gaining intimate familiarity with initial public offerings, mergers and acquisitions, and hostile takeover attempts that were the Wall Street rage in those days.

By my third rotation, I had proved sufficiently competent as a draftsman and sufficiently sound in my judgments that I was given additional responsibilities. I drafted partnership and joint venture agreements for IBM, junk bond offerings for Citicorp Securities, and the documents for Morgan Stanley when it created an auction sale for a subsidiary of a major manufacturing conglomerate. I was certainly finding my feet. In fact, every added increment of responsibility found me better prepared, more confident—whatever the setting, whatever the situation, however experienced or highly paid the opposing counsel might be.

But as special and as precious as the education was, it left me a troubled student, stirring in me misgivings that would not go away and could not be denied. Despite my respect for my colleagues, my arguments with myself, and the rewards I enjoyed as a $175,000-a-year associate, my unease persisted. At first, it all had to do with money.

The amounts of money spent in the process of executing an IPO, or effecting a merger, or fighting a hostile takeover struck me as staggering. And the cavalier attitude with which the money was spent made me uncomfortable. Time and again, I ran into high-priced lawyers and investment bankers who never thought twice about doling out huge chunks of other people's money as if it were their own. The team was working late and needed dinner? Call the four-star restaurant in the next block and have it delivered. One of the partners had left a file at his weekend estate in the Hamptons? Order a limousine to retrieve it. Time to make a presentation to the client? Hire a team of top-notch multimedia consultants. After all, in the end, it's all the client's money.

So on the client's money, we flew on the Concorde, we stayed at the grandest hotels, we dined in the most sumptuous restaurants. It was nothing remarkable to set off on a trip holding $20,000's worth of airline tickets, to check in at the Connaught in London, the Ritz in Paris, to lunch at Wilton's, the Tour d'Argent, or the Four Seasons. The scale of the expense account confirmed my suspicion that, to lawyers and their clients, money equaled authority. The more money at stake, the more we spent; the more we spent, the more brilliant we could be confident we were.

One could argue, of course, that these expenditures were justified. When people are spending nights and weekends at work—night after night, weekend after weekend—it makes sense to feed them well. When a file is needed, it's needed. Period. If it has been accidentally left behind, the important thing is to get it here fast. As to creating a world-class presentation, we were, after all, a world-class law firm; it was entirely fitting that the medium as well as the message should be highly professional.

Moreover, given the amounts of money involved in most of the deals we were effecting—hundreds of millions of dollars, even billions—the thousands spent on expenses seemed a trifle. Given what was at stake, our expense sheet was not disproportionate.

So it might have been argued to me, and so I kept telling myself. Despite the one-way conversation, however, a worm of doubt was beginning to crawl around in my gut. The worm really turned the first time I worked on an IPO.

. . .

On its face, an IPO is a pretty simple affair. A company that needs to raise capital decides to sell shares of ownership in itself to the public. It is betting that its product or service, its management and culture, its performance and prospects will prove attractive enough to investors that a sufficient number of them will want to own a piece of the action.

While it sounds pretty straightforward in theory, in practice the IPO tends to be a fairly complicated affair. What kind of securities should the company issue? At what price? With what special features? How much will it cost? These are just some of the issues that must be resolved before the company can even begin to raise capital.

Then there is the regulatory gauntlet: the registration statements and disclosures and complete financial statements to be filed with the right agency in the right way at just the right time.

Next, it's necessary to drum up interest in the company so that investors will buy shares in it. This requires the creation of a prospectus that describes what the company is and does, who runs it, how it has performed, and what it intends to do with the money it raises.

Then somebody actually has to go out and beat the bushes to find investors and get them to commit to taking a certain percentage of the public offering. Stockbrokers have to be brought onboard, so that they can help move the stock to the general public once the offering has been made. And it all has to be timed right—both to meet regulatory requirements and to affect the market in the right way—and not a single detail can be overlooked.

In other words, there is a fair amount that must happen between a company's decision to go public and the moment the stock actually hits the market. Managing it all is the job of an investment bank. It acts as advisor on the process and as distributor of the offering. It underwrites the stock issue and handles the actual process of raising capital. Helping it do all this is a team of lawyers, and among the most renowned Wall Street lawyers are the men and women of Cravath, Swaine & Moore, which has been helping investment banks take companies public for more than a century.

The first IPO I worked on was a big one. It involved some ten Cravath lawyers working flat out—each with a meter running at hundreds of dollars an hour per head. Their staff of associates—young lawyers like me—worked even longer hours, doing the grunt work, the research, the particulars. Our job was to check and recheck every detail and challenge every word in the prospectus. The idea was to make it foolproof, so that the client would be free of the risk of any sort of lawsuit.

The endgame of the process for us was when lawyers and staff assembled at the financial printing company, the esteemed R. R. Donnelley, printers to the financial industry almost the way British firms are "by appointment" to the Queen.

I well remember the first time I entered the elaborate Donnelley offices, located since time immemorial in the narrow canyons of lower Manhattan. I joined a dozen other young Cravath associates in a locked but luxurious conference room. There, presumably hidden from unscrupulous investors, we scrutinized every detail of the prospectus in safety and security. A large television screen and a regulation-sized pool table were there to help us relax when we needed a breather. Messengers swirled in and out rushing important papers back and forth to estates in Connecticut and penthouses on Fifth Avenue. Limousines delivered our individual orders for expensive dinners, all courtesy of the printing company, which of course charged it back to the client. I remember that one of the lawyers casually asked for a beer. A Donnelley operative departed instantly for the nearest deli, returning half an hour later with a dozen beers on a tray, each of them already opened. Which one would the lawyer like? he wanted to know.

Not for the first time, I began to wonder who was getting what out of all this—and who was paying for it. The printers, quite obviously, were making a fortune. They adored new issues, when they were called upon to produce, package, and distribute the prospectus simultaneously to hundreds of thousands of brokers all over the United States and often the rest of the world. From a highly automated hub, the printers fanned the work out to a network of satellite plants that finished the production and handled the distribution. Printing bills not infrequently reached a million dollars or more—and nobody balked.

We the lawyers were also being handsomely paid, not to mention the fact that our time at the printers was equivalent to living on room service in a four-star hotel without ever paying the bill. But puffed up as I felt on that first IPO, I also sensed that there was something off-key about its cost. The locked room, the luxurious meals, the enormity of the printing bill all fed the perception that we were very important people. I wondered.

Then there were the investment bankers, among the top winners in an IPO process. Their big moment came when they took the prospectus on the road, shopping the issue to certain preferred institutions and very, very wealthy individual investors. To make sure they sold the issue, the investment bankers offered these institutions and individuals two things that were not available to the public at large.

First, they made the price of the issue so attractive that the preferred investors would snap it up. Second, they offered them information that was not in the prospectus and that the public would therefore never learn. The prospectus, after all, the document so many of us at Cravath had labored over so long and hard, is really a defensive document. It is aimed at satisfying the disclosure requirements of the Securities and Exchange Commission and warding off later lawsuits by angry investors. In a prospectus, you can't say anything about how you think the company will do once it has raised the capital or what the analysts think of its future financial projections. But once they were on the road, the investment bankers and the executives of the issuing company could say exactly that, as they conferred with the institutional buyers in private meetings where note-taking was not allowed.

This kind of information, plus an enticing low offering price, usually did the trick. The institutional and wealthy individual investors would commit to buy, ensuring that the issue would appear on the stock market. Once it did, the preferred buyers, the institutional investors, assisted by retail brokers who promote the stocks to their regular customers, flip the stock at big profits to them—not to the company.

What's more, putting on the road show to drum up the big-money institutional investors was incredibly costly. Jetloads of company executives and investment bankers spent weeks racing around the country—sometimes the globe—making one presentation after another. No expense was spared. After all, if a company set out to float, say, $100 million in new stock, its managers would soon be awash in new money, and the underwriters would make 7 percent on the deal. Among company management, lawyers, and investment bankers—all of whom were living off the fat of the land to make the offering happen—nobody seemed at all inclined to blow the whistle on the process.

That's the way it all proceeded on my first IPO. At the closing dinner, when the lead investment banker stood up suddenly, raised his glass, and asked us to toast the fact that the new issue had leapt 38 percent above the offering price in a single day of public trading, I saw the company president nearly drop his glass, heard the chief financial officer gulp, and watched the vice president's face fall.

And who could blame them? The investment bankers had assured company management that the low stock price offered to all those preferred investors was the best they could get, the highest the preferred customers would pay. Accept that price, they had advised the company, or see the issue fail. As soon as the IPO reached the public, however, with buzz and hype by ordinary stock brokers paving the way, eager retail buyers had snapped at it, trading up the price. No wonder the investment bankers were toasting their own good fortune and that of their preferred customers, while the issuing company and, above all, the investing public were getting the short end of the stick.

It was *their* money—the investing public's money—that had been squandered on lawyers and bankers, on Lear jets and limos, on restaurants and road shows. As the new shareholders of the company, they were its real owners. Yet nobody had given them much thought at all—not at any point during the lavish IPO process, and not at the closing dinner in the elegant surroundings open only to a privileged few.

Despite the surroundings, however, I felt ill at ease. I could swallow the tournedos Rossini, but something else was stuck in my craw that even the fine Médoc could not wash down. It wasn't just the way money was thrown around on the client's behalf and at his expense, but the underlying purpose of the work I had just done on this IPO.

Who were these giant investment banks for whom I had toiled so loyally? What about the giant multinational to which our Cravath team had been billing tens of thousands of dollars a day? I was no wide-eyed idealist, to be sure. I had known, when I signed on at Cravath, that I was not dedicating myself to serving the poor, or even to serving the public. But in this huge institutional process I had just been through, wealth had been created through the engineering of complex financial transactions. My team of lawyers had pushed some papers here and some other papers there, and money had flowed to people who were already enormously rich. As to the entrepreneurs and workers who had built the company in the first place, as to the people who had created the idea, found the backing, invented the products, taken the chances, and worked the long hours, where were they? And where was their payoff?

I wasn't the first young lawyer to feel disillusionment. "Trade-offs" were a favorite topic of conversation among the associates gunning for partner. We were on track for the Park Avenue apartment, the summerhouse at the beach, the African safari vacation, the expensive schools for the children we didn't yet have. Would it all prove to be worth the malaise we were beginning to feel as we helped yet another soulless institution effect yet another acquisition, or merger, or secured loan transaction? That was our work, and it was what paid for the life we thought we wanted. But the misgivings persisted. They made me question whether I really wanted that life after all.

One day, a senior associate who had become a friend of mine at Cravath found himself crying when he learned he had made partner. Now he knew, he told me, that he was trapped. He could no longer pretend that he could still get out, still do something else with his life. It set me to thinking.

In the midst of these half-baked, still amorphous concerns, something rather distracting occurred: I fell in love.

3.

Love in New and Old Amsterdam

In the spring of 1989, a beautiful Dutch woman named Liesbeth, on leave from graduate studies at the University of Amsterdam and working on a temporary basis at the United Nations New York headquarters, agreed to spend a day driving in the Hudson Valley. That evening, we ate pizza at Stromboli's near New York University, and later we went bowling at Bowlmor Lanes right next door. We have been together ever since.

Falling in love with Liesbeth did not make my misgivings about my work life disappear, but it did help put them into perspective. What mattered now was how much I hated to think about Liesbeth's having to return to her studies in Amsterdam. That summer, we took a month's vacation together in Indonesia, and when I returned to Cravath, and she returned to Holland in September, my main objective in life was finding a way for us to be together. We agreed that, somehow, I would try to get transferred to Cravath's London office, a lot closer than New Amsterdam to old Amsterdam.

At the time, Cravath's London office was a small operation, staffed by only six lawyers, for all of whom the London assignment was a long-awaited, much-worked-for plum. I put myself on the waiting list, however, along with scores of others who yearned for London duty. Realistically, I might get my turn in a couple of years, if I were really lucky.

So it was startling, to say the least, when one week after I applied, a senior partner walked into my office, introduced himself, and said, "I hear you want to go to London."

My heart was pounding. "I would love to go to London," I said.

"How soon can you leave?" the partner asked me.

"Immediately," I answered.

"What about Monday?" he asked. This was Wednesday.

"Of course," I replied. "No problem."

"Go home and pack," said the partner.

That's just what I did. I packed up everything I owned over the weekend, sublet my apartment on Sunday, and flew to London on Monday. Meanwhile, Liesbeth managed to convince her thesis advisor that she needed to be in London to do research on her topic. Within a week, Liesbeth joined me in a flat off the Kings Road in London's Chelsea district, where we lived happily for the next two years.

Not that we had much time to be together. Cravath had a client with an urgent need, and I had been seconded to London to help. I was there as a foot soldier, manning the trenches in defense of the London-based conglomerate known as BAT Industries against a hostile takeover attempt by the colorful corporate raider, Sir James Goldsmith. One of the renowned takeover artists of the 1980s—and later portrayed, slimly disguised and not wholly without sympathy, in Oliver Stone's movie *Wall Street*—Goldsmith had a well-known modus operandi. He would simply buy up vulnerable companies, break them apart, then sell the pieces for millions more than his original purchase price.

His latest target, Cravath's client, BAT, was a transatlantic colossus that embraced a variety of American companies, including a large insurance operation called the Farmers Group Inc. At the time that Goldsmith targeted BAT, its market value was approximately $18 billion. Goldsmith aimed to earn himself a great deal more than $18 billion by selling pieces of BAT. Step one, of course, was to buy the conglomerate, which Goldsmith intended to do simply by offering BAT shareholders more money for their company in a tender offer than the shares were then trading for on the stock market. Cravath's job, our job in the London office, my job—was to make Sir James go away so that the shareholders never had a chance to make a choice between his tender offer and current management. The task at hand consisted of coming up with a long list of tactics that could at worst slow and at best completely thwart the pursuit of the tender offer.

First, we managed to get the regulators of Britain's stock market to niggle over a number of purely technical details. That alone cost everybody a lot of money and delayed the process considerably, although it did not actually kill it. Then we turned to the United States, where our federal system presented the pleasing fact of fifteen separate insurance commissions regulating the Farmers Group, one commission for each of the fifteen states in which the insurance company did business. For Goldsmith to acquire the Farmers Group, he would need permission from each of those states. Surely, one regulator on one commission could find one reason to veto the transaction. One was all that was needed.

Cravath put together a nationwide network of lawyers, publicists, and lobbyists to find the one. Millions of dollars were spent on the effort—money well spent, as it ultimately turned out. My part in the Battle of the Insurance Commissioners was waged first in BAT's London headquarters, where I had been dispatched to help BAT's general counsel coordinate the worldwide effort aimed at fighting the battle through local counsel in the fifteen states.

For almost a year, we spent up to six hours a day every day on international conference calls. Even on leased lines and across proprietary communications networks, the cost of our efforts was staggering, and we were just one small front in the war.

In the midst of the battle, I was handed a new assignment in the insurance offensive—this one in Paris. The firm had come up with the somewhat disingenuous defense that Goldsmith was unfit to run an insurance company. Goldsmith had countered this assertion by getting a large French insurance company, Axa Midi, to agree to buy Farmers Group as soon as he took over BAT. My job was to fly to Paris, rent a three-room suite at the elegant Plaza-Athenée Hotel, and dig through every conceivable source of dirt on Claude Bebeare, the distinguished chairman of Axa Midi. The right hint of scandal would presumably convince U.S. regulators that Axa Midi was unfit to own the Farmers Group, thus wrecking Goldsmith's entire BAT bid.

From the plushest of plush settings, I looked as hard as I could for something vile, contemptible, or corrupt. I didn't find it. Bebeare proved to be dirt-free. I found nobody willing to say that he beat his children, milked his shareholders, cheated his policyholders, or committed any other unseemly acts.

My colleagues back in the States, however, had found the veto they needed. After a remarkable performance by a whole regiment of lawyers, the top brass of Cravath's litigation team managed to convince California's insurance regulators that the Farmers Group would be in unsafe hands if acquired by Goldsmith. What wowed the regulators was a potential "gap" in the transfer agreement that might find Sir James owning BAT but Axa Midi backing out of its commitment to purchase Farmers. That remote but technically possible eventuality was enough for the regulators to nix the entire transaction.

Within weeks of this stunning victory, the junk bond market, on which Sir James was relying to finance his bid, collapsed suddenly. A month later, he dropped the whole takeover effort.

The precipitate end of the BAT wars caught me by surprise and left me feeling somewhat dislocated. I had spent weeks in Paris on a generous expense account, living it up, and rather hoping the party would never end. At the same time, I was twenty-nine years old, uncomfortable with the values I was being overpaid to advance, and increasingly aware that I ought to be focusing my life on something healthier.

I had gone to Paris, after all, on the shareholders' dollars, to dig for dirt on a perfectly honorable entrepreneur. The point in doing so was to defeat the legitimate aspirations of another businessman, who intended nothing more or less than to offer these shareholders more money than the market reflected. Why were BAT managers free to plunder the corporate treasury just to try to keep the shareholders from considering any Goldsmith offer for their stock, even an offer they could refuse? If Goldsmith was indeed bad for BAT, as the managers claimed, shouldn't the managers make their case, let Goldsmith make his, and let the shareholders decide? After all, wasn't it the shareholders who owned the company? Shouldn't they have a shot at choosing? They. The shareholders. The very people who, unbeknownst to them, were cushioning me from the difficulties of such thoughts with the most luxurious pampering money could buy. My job here had not been to protect them, or to advance the value of their holdings. My job had been to save the hides of corporate management and give them job security—at least until the next hostile takeover attempt.

It was the spring of 1991. I had been at Cravath for six years. Certainly, the one thing in my life that was completely healthy was my relationship with Liesbeth. She, too, seemed to be at a kind of crossroads. Having completed her thesis, she found herself unexcited about the prospects for meaningful work in London.

One night, dining on sushi in a little restaurant near Covent Garden, we fell together on a great idea. We decided we had both worked hard enough the past two years. It was time for a time out, for travel, for fun, for being together. I took a leave of absence from the firm, we bought one-way air tickets to Bombay, and off we went. For six months we wandered through India, Nepal, and China. The Taj Mahal. Everest base camp at Annapurna. The Great Wall. Amid the exotic sights and sounds of these fabled destinations, places that would fire any imagination, my worries and misgivings subsided.

It was getting on for summer as the six months of wandering drew to a close. Liesbeth and I headed for Holland. We had decided to get married. Now was the time, and Amsterdam was the place.

Summer is Holland's best season, the one time of year when the weather is reliably fine, and that summer was a particularly golden one. We were surrounded by family and friends in what seemed a summerlong party, much of it spent sitting around in the city's delightful open-air cafés, along with thousands of relaxed Dutch people. At the same time, we were on the threshold of the most important commitment two people can make in life, a statement of optimism about the possibilities of the future if ever there was one. It was an exceptionally happy time. Exhilarating. Great fun. And everywhere we looked that glorious summer, Amsterdamers were nursing heavy jam jars filled with an unusual drink. It looked odd—blondish, cloudy, with a wedge of lemon skewered with a stirring rod—but it tasted great: light, slightly citrusy, with absolutely no bitter aftertaste. I learned it was an old Belgian-recipe beer, what the Flemish called *witbier.*

4.

Time Out for Inspiration

Inspiration? In a book about capital formation and securities offerings and Internet technology?

In fact, nothing is more central to a business enterprise—*any* business enterprise—than that stimulation of the mind, that stirring of the intellect that enlivens an individual to set in motion something new. Business success, like all human progress, comes from the breakthrough idea, the fresh discovery, the original creation—all the result of a moment of inspiration.

But inspiration can rarely be summoned at will. You can't command it to start working. Like love, inspiration comes when you least expect it. When you're not looking for it. When you think there's no particular need for it. In that summer of love in Amsterdam, inspiration came to me in a split second, in a perfectly ordinary setting, in the most normal, everyday set of circumstances. It was an epiphany, and I recognized it as such the moment it occurred. I knew that something important had happened, that something fundamental in my life had changed. What I did not know was where it would lead.

The conventional wisdom is that you're supposed to get increasingly nervous as your wedding day draws near, but I was entirely relaxed and having a wonderful time. Part of this might have been attributed to the *witbier*—"vit-beer," as it's pronounced in the Low Countries. It was certainly unlike any beer I had ever had before. As refreshing as a glass of lemonade but with a soft yet spicy "kick," I learned that it was a centuries-old Belgian beer, originally brewed from wheat. In fact, *wit* means "wheat," although later, the meaning of *witbier* was extended to "white beer," a reference to the pale, cloudy appearance of the brew. I also learned that *witbier*'s spicy taste came from a unique blend of Spanish orange peels and coriander brewed directly into the beer.

In London a decade earlier, I had acquired a taste for the full-bodied ales, the dark stouts, and the stinging pale ales that have long defined British brewing. But this was summer. Even dark-ale loyalists will admit that in the heat of summer, you sometimes need a cold, light, thirst-quenching drink. *Witbier*.

Among the friends who had come for the wedding was Russell, a skilled, charismatic soccer player I had met in London back in 1989. Russell was a native New Zealander; in fact, he descends from the original natives, the Maori. He was a colorful character and a good friend, and he was a man who knew a good beer when he drank one.

So when he arrived in Amsterdam shortly before the wedding, it was only natural that I should introduce him to my new discovery. It was another lovely, sunny day. Russell and I were seated outside at a café. The waiter approached. *"Twee witbieren, alstublieft,"* I said. Two *witbiers*, please.

Russell looked dubious when the *witbier* was set before him. "Hmm. Odd one, isn't it," he said.

"Tastes irresistible, though," I countered. "Give it a try."

Russell gave it a try. He sipped, swallowed, and sighed contentedly. Then he tried it again.

I was right. Russell had not been able to resist *witbier*. At that moment, a lightbulb switched on.

"Russell," I heard myself saying, "I'm going to bring this beer to America."

As revelations go, mine was hardly on a par with Moses receiving the Ten Commandments on Sinai. Nevertheless, when I made my announcement to Russell, I recognized it as a serious statement, one that resonated persuasively in my mind. The next day, without being entirely sure where I was headed, I began building a beer company.

5.

You Have to Start Somewhere

I'm going to bring witbier *to America*, I had heard myself proclaim—a piece of grandiloquence that was about as far-fetched as it could be. So far from being in a position to build my own company, I was little more than a worker bee in someone else's company. I earned my daily bread by making it possible for distant entrepreneurs to take their companies public, which was a long way from being an entrepreneur myself. What's more, I hadn't a glimmer of an idea how to go about building a company that would sell *witbier.* In fact, however, my ignorance may have been the best thing that could have happened to me.

For one thing, I didn't know enough to have any doubts. Having no idea about what might lie ahead—how much work, how many disappointments—I simply assumed that it was possible to introduce *witbier* in the United States successfully, and that I was perfectly equipped to do it.

For another thing, I knew so little that I wasn't afraid to ask what might have been considered dumb questions. I was also entirely open to fresh ideas, new ways of doing things. The polite way of putting it is to say that I had no preconceived notions; when you're at ground zero, the only direction is up.

Ground zero that autumn of 1991, however, was pretty high: My new office at Cravath was on the forty-ninth floor. Yes, I was back. Newly wed. With several months of refreshing world travel behind me. Just off the plane from a round of joyous parties during that Amsterdam summer. By any measure, I should have been a man eager to plunge back into preventing hostile takeovers and smoothing the way for initial securities offerings.

I was anything but. From my office window, I could look due west over the rooftops of Manhattan across the Hudson River to New Jersey. The view offered a panorama of rooftops, traffic, and, occasionally, a tugboat pushing a garbage scow up or down the river. Yet, feet on my desk, I contemplated all this for hours on end while my in-basket filled up with business that no longer intrigued me. What did intrigue me was my passion to bring *witbier* to America.

The first thing I did was head to the library. Under the letter *b* for beer, I began to research my subject. I read voraciously. I learned more about beer than I would ever have believed there was to learn.

One of the first things I learned was that Moses may indeed have been drinking beer when he climbed up Sinai to receive the Commandments. In fact, beer making—and beer drinking—go back at least 6,000 years and have their origin in the Middle East. It was in ancient Sumeria, in the famed "cradle of civilization" between the Tigris and Euphrates rivers, that the fermentation process was accidentally discovered. Maybe a breadmaker got caught in a downpour, forgot about the bread, and when she remembered it, found it had an exciting taste and left an exciting impression. The result was a drink that made people feel "exhilarated, wonderful, and blissful," according to a Sumerian inscription. The Babylonians agreed; they learned to brew twenty different types of beer, while their great lawmaker, Hammurabi, established a daily beer ration, based on rank, and prescribed drowning as the punishment for serving low-quality beer.

From the Middle East, the beer idea spread far and wide—north and west around the Mediterranean, up through Europe, on into present-day Scandinavia and beyond. In addition to its taste and effect, beer had other advantages: it was far less perishable than most foods, safer to drink than the water from ancient water sources, and was believed to increase health, cure malnutrition, and enhance longevity. By the ninth century, a number of breweries had sprung up, and brewers had begun to add bitter and aromatic herbs, roots, and flowers to flavor beer as well as to help preserve it. Among the many ingredients used as flavorings in these recipe beers were juniper berries, rosemary, spruce chips, pine roots, bay leaves, blackthorn, oak bark, aniseed, caraway seed, thorn apple, gentian, even wormwood. In time, breweries would concoct their own flavoring recipes, closely guarded commercial secrets that governments eventually licensed as monopolies.

Originally the province of women, beer brewing became a manly art in the Middle Ages when the monasteries of Europe took it up. But it was a woman, Abbess Hildegard—later Saint Hildegard—who first added hop flowers to the brewing process, a move that was to have dramatic and far-reaching consequences. Hops helped stabilize and preserve beer brews, and that, in turn, made beer more viable commercially—easier to distribute, even to export. At the same time, the hops softened the bitter sourness of most primitive beer. This reduced the need for all those exotic flavorings, which led to a fairly uniform beer recipe—and a fairly uniform beer taste.

But while the popularity of spiced and flavored beers diminished, they never entirely died out. In the eastern provinces of Belgium, in fact, a number of ancient beer styles remained popular well into the modern era. And *witbier*, first recorded in the records kept by early beer historians some five hundred years ago, was the most popular of them all. Its unique recipe may have originated as a simple, practical response to the abundance of wheat grown in Europe five hundred years ago, and to the brisk trade carried out by Flemish traders who routinely brought home oranges from Spain and spices from the East Indies. Whether by enterprise or by accident, orange peel and coriander were combined, the combination proved popular, and the recipe soon became a hit with brewers—and beer drinkers—all across the Low Countries. By the 1800s, in fact, there were nearly a hundred breweries producing *witbier* throughout the northern provinces of what is today Belgium.

As the popularity of hop-flavored brewing grew, however, Belgian brewers found themselves squeezed between the two powers that had perfected it, England and Germany, and they had to fight for even a declining share of older drinkers still loyal to their cloudy brews.

At the same time, technological advances made wheat more appropriate for bread baking and advanced the use of barley for beer brewing. The result was that Belgian brewers increasingly turned to barley-based beers spiced with hops, and the popularity of *witbier* diminished.

By the latter part of the nineteenth century, the number of *witbier* brands in production had dwindled to a handful. By the middle of the twentieth century, there were only two. And just a few years later, the last of the *witbier* breweries disappeared altogether when an infection spread through all the remaining wooden brewing vats and spoiled the yeast strains that produced the special *witbier* taste. In 1954, with the last of the original *witbier* breweries closed and locked, the beer style itself entered the ranks of endangered species. *Witbier* was now only a memory, and even the memory was vanishing fast.

Enter Pierre Celis, an enterprising milkman in the tiny village of Hoegaarden, site of one of the last *witbier* breweries. The Celis family had lived next door to the brewery, and Pierre Celis had grown up with the sounds, smells, and taste of *witbier* production as his closest companions. He sorely missed the old drink.

For years, Pierre lamented the dear, departed past of *witbier*. To anyone who would listen, he held forth on the subject, declaring his deeply held conviction that somebody ought to resurrect the old brewing methods and the old *witbier* brew. One day in early 1966, Pierre Celis stopped lamenting and decided that he could be that somebody. He quit his job as a milkman, gathered together some makeshift equipment, rented a 400-square-foot garage, and had himself a *witbier* brewery. He called the brand Hoegaarden.

Local pubs were the first to serve it. Then, as word spread from village to village throughout the province, orders mounted. In time,

Hoegaarden *witbier* became famous throughout the country and beyond, drawing beer enthusiasts from around the world to the little brewery in the little village. And Pierre Celis walked off with the honor of having saved *witbier* from extinction.

In 1975, Celis joined forces with an admiring Flemish businessman who had made a fortune in bottling soda. The businessman liked the beer enough to provide capital and distribution channels and a plan to market *witbier* in mainstream markets throughout Belgium and other parts of Europe.

The partnership built a larger brewery and redesigned the packaging material. Sure enough, *witbier* began showing up on menus at the trendiest cafés frequented by the trendiest young people in Brussels, Antwerp, and other towns and cities around Belgium.

It wasn't long before imitations appeared on the market. By the early 1980s, several small breweries were marketing *witbier* throughout the country. The *witbier* style soon qualified as a distinct category of beer; within a few years, it was a category that accounted for nearly 5 percent of all beers consumed in Belgium. And not just Belgium, either. One Dutch version, called Witte Raaf, was founded by a skillful brewer named Herm Hegger. Remember the name; it will figure prominently in my story.

With the proliferation of small breweries, it wasn't long before the big breweries sat up and took notice of the *witbier* revival. Unhappily for this story, Pierre Celis missed out on the big payoff he so richly deserved. A fire destroyed his inadequately insured brewery just at the time that his brew, Hoegaarden, was emerging as the top brand. Unable to rebuild, Celis was in a weak position when he sold the Hoegaarden brand name to Interbrew, Belgium's top beer marketer. It was a difficult and sad move for Celis, but it proved to be a clarion call to other major brewers. Holland's Heineken, for one, quickly caught on and bought a rival brand, Wieckse Witte, to combat Interbrew's move. The Heineken initiative in its turn unplugged the Dutch beer dike, releasing the great *witbier* flood that was washing all through the north countries of Europe.

The flood had seemed to me to be cresting that past summer in

Amsterdam. Back in New York, high above the busy Manhattan streets, the new assignments piled up in my mailbox while I brooded on beer. *Witbier. Witbier* in America, for Americans.

In Holland, everything had converged at just the right time, in just the right way: a microbrewery boom, aggressive marketing, the revival and reconfiguration of the old brew. It seemed that *witbier* could not have come along at a better moment. With its roots in the past and its contemporary, fresh, jaunty taste, it offered a formula that seemed perfect for a time of prosperity, an era of confidence, a generation eager to reap the rewards of life and willing to pay a premium for them. That's why *witbier* had dominated the fashionable cafés of Amsterdam that summer. But did it have a chance over here? I toted up the possibilities.

First, the product itself was outstanding—rare and intriguing, attributes that would appeal to an important niche of the American market.

Then there was the story, at once powerful and charming: an ancient recipe on the edge of extinction rescued by a milkman.

Moreover, as a natural, handcrafted product, *witbier* would be very attractive to that growing crowd of consumers tired of mass-produced food products. These consumers were spending millions on specialty or "designer" foods—premium ice creams, gourmet breads, boutique wines. They were also beginning to spend on a growing microbrewing industry. From the Northwest to New England, pockets of microbrewers were fomenting revolution as they fermented quality beers. Within this nascent trend, *witbier* was something special: a full-flavored beer that was not bitter-tasting. The perfect alternative for beer drinkers who loved the idea of micro-brewed beer but had found the products thus far to be too difficult a taste to acquire. Or for light beer drinkers who wanted to advance to specialty tastes but not if they had to hold their noses and force it down. Or even for the white wine drinkers who appreciated everything about beer except the taste.

Witbier would appeal to all these people, I thought, and of course it would also appeal to serious beer drinkers eager, as always, for a wonderful new brew.

Forty-ninth-floor fantasies—or a serious business possibility?

I sensed that the moment was as ripe in America as it was in Belgium and Holland, that the appeal of *witbier* would cross the ocean and beguile people in the New World as in the Old. Was I right? Could I capitalize on the *witbier* phenomenon that seemed evident all over Amsterdam that idyllic summer? One thing was for certain: I had no idea how.

So one day that September, I took my feet off the desk, picked up the telephone, and called my brother-in-law in Amsterdam. "Please, Eddie," I begged, "do me a favor and go shopping. Buy one bottle of every *witbier* brand sold in Holland, and send them all to me in New York." Eddie did exactly that. I sifted through the labels on the bottles for all the information they could yield and culled enough to create a *witbier* database on my home computer. I then sent a form letter to each of the brewers in my database. The letters claimed that I was writing on behalf of a group of highly experienced New York importers I had the good fortune to represent. These importers, I asserted, were most eager to sell the brewer's superb product here in the United States. What we needed, most urgently, was a sample batch of the product and permission to test the product here in the immense and surely receptive U.S. market. I ended by assuring them that success on a vast scale was all but guaranteed.

If the contents of the letter stretched the truth a bit, the letter's impact more than counterbalanced the transgression: Absolutely nothing happened.

Late summer segued into a brisk, beautiful autumn. Autumn ended abruptly with a fierce cold snap and a heavy snowfall. My duties at Cravath engulfed my time. If I had not entirely given up the idea of importing *witbier*, I was close. A passion that evokes no response will eventually be preempted, and my life was indeed beginning to be filled with other things.

Then one cold February morning in 1992, the phone rang, and a slightly accented male voice announced, "My name is Herm Hegger. I brew *witbier*. You wrote me a letter."

Indeed I had. Herm Hegger had learned the art of *witbier* brewing in Belgium when the *witbier* craze was just getting under way. He had parlayed that expertise into the creation of his own *witbier* brand for the Dutch market, Witte Raaf (it means "white raven"), which had since become the fourth largest brand in Holland. When the major breweries began to invade the *witbier* market, Hegger quickly saw the handwriting on the wall and put Raaf up for sale. His timing for getting out of the market was as savvy as his timing for getting in, and Hegger had just completed the sale of Raaf to one of the majors when he phoned me. "I'm no longer in a position to export *witbier*," he told me, "but I certainly know how to make *witbier*, if you ever consider going that route."

In addition to being the only nibble I had received in six months, Herm Hegger's suggestion was one of those fresh new ideas to which my status as a novice in the beer business made me receptive. I immediately requested a week's vacation, and Liesbeth and I grabbed the next plane to Amsterdam.

On arrival, we borrowed my mother-in-law's car and headed for the little village of Heumen. It was here that the Raaf brewery was located, and it was here that Hegger lived, in an old farmhouse just on the edge of the village.

To say that Herm and I hit it off is an understatement. Rather, it was as if we had known each other for years but had just been waiting to meet. That afternoon, Liesbeth and I basked in the Hegger hospitality as Herm gave us a first-person account of the Raaf brewery and the entire *witbier* phenomenon. As interesting as Herm's description of *witbier*'s past success was his conviction that such success could continue—and that it could certainly cross the ocean. By the end of the day, Herm and I had agreed to join forces and make *witbier* in the United States.

Herm was the perfect partner. He was a master *witbier* brewer. He had no job and was committed to no other projects. The sale of his brewery had netted enough to make him financially independent. His interest in partnering with me was born of an entrepreneurial spirit and a shared passion for *witbier*. As if that weren't enough, we liked each other enormously. That was the icing on the cake. It made Herm Hegger the answer to my prayers.

We formalized the agreement about a month later, in early April 1992. Herm flew to New York—his first visit ever—and met me at Cravath headquarters on a surreal Saturday afternoon. What made the day surreal was not the weather, which was still cool and a bit drab, or our meeting, which was as friendly on this side of the Atlantic as when we had said farewell in Heumen. What lent drama to the afternoon was what was going on around Herm and me as we concluded our agreement. Some particularly cosmic takeover battle was under way—I no longer remember the details—and hordes of combative lawyers had jammed into the firm's conference rooms to fight it. There were quite literally hundreds of lawyers present, not to mention support personnel of every stripe, and the comings and goings, the arguments and discussions, the noise of copy machines and faxes and telephones all made the place look, feel, and sound like Grand Central Station at rush hour. In the midst of it all, Herm and I commandeered an empty corner, negotiated a partnership agreement, and drafted a contract. I was putting my signature to some piece of paper when I realized we needed a name for the company we were founding, so I quickly put my middle name into service and we created the Douglas Beer Company. In exchange for stock in Douglas Beer, Herm would provide his recipes and services for three years. We were partners.

The assets of the partnership at that time were twofold: We had the recipe, and we knew how to make the beer. Now all we needed was some place where we could make our beer our way. That need immediately put us up against our first reality and spurred our first business decision. The reality was that history and our own resources limited our choices in finding a brewery. We certainly could not afford to build a brewery; we had neither the money nor the time for that. Nor could we buy a brewery; even if we had the money for such a purchase, we couldn't just call up a brewery broker, state our needs, and wait for a listing of available facilities. America had changed: the once-ubiquitous local brewery was now almost as rare as the local livery stable.

It was a fairly recent change. Throughout most of the century, the United States had practically foamed with beer companies. Every town had its local brewery. Fair-sized towns had more than one. Brooklyn in the heyday of local beer brewing boasted twenty-seven breweries; Manhattan had fourteen. And each of these brews had its own distinctive taste. Variety ruled. As recently as thirty years ago, an American beer drinker had his or her pick of all manner of ale, lager, and stout.

That began to change in the 1960s. Such technological advances as refrigerated shipping and the kinds of nationwide marketing the chain supermarkets were devising all led to a period of consolidation in beer brewing. The national brands like Budweiser and Miller, capitalizing on the economies of scale they could achieve, were able to cover bigger and bigger markets, and eventually they all but obliterated the regional and local breweries. By the early 1970s, only four major breweries produced nearly 95 percent of all the beer made in the United States.

That was the situation that confronted Herm and me. With no brewery to buy, and with no wherewithal to build a brewery, what were we to do?

"Why not become contract brewers?" suggested Herm. In other words, do a deal with a larger brewery to produce our beer according to our own recipe, under Herm's supervision, using the brewery's facilities and brewing expertise. It was a good idea, and one reason we knew it was good was that it had been tried before. In fact, contract brewing had fueled the extraordinary growth of microbrewing.

Microbrewing was a reaction to the loss of diversity that resulted from the consolidation of the brewing industry. As the major national brands aspired to milder and milder tastes to appeal to some sort of national least common denominator, two things happened: the beer all began to taste the same, and it all began to taste lousy. A *Consumer's Research* taste test in the late 1970s found that Bud drinkers couldn't tell their brew from Miller and vice versa. All you had to do was sip either one of them to know that, where taste is concerned, nondescript means bad.

That homogenization, in turn, led to a backlash, as challengers saw an opportunity to distinguish themselves in the marketplace by offering diverse beer styles, richer in taste and higher in quality. Producing beer in small quantities, these microbrewers began to turn out what was called specialty beer, gourmet beer, or, in the jargon of the times, craft beer.

In fact, the early microbrewers were small pubs in the Pacific Northwest where the beer was made and sold right on the premises. Each microbrew tended to develop its own loyal following. In time, the best of them grew into full-scale breweries that sold their beers to other pubs, bars, and restaurants, then to upmarket gourmet stores and, eventually, the chain supermarkets.

The most successful microbrewer, however, was not a pub owner in the Northwest but a Harvard-educated management consultant in Massachusetts. Jim Koch, a graduate of the Harvard Business School and a consultant with the prestigious Boston Consulting Group, was the son, grandson, and great-grandson of beer brewers. Family legend talked of Great-Granddad's secret recipe for a special beer, stored somewhere up in the attic, but it took Jim's B-school training and marketing savvy to realize the potential of the old recipe. And what prompted Koch to dust off his great-grandfather's formula was not so much his beer heritage as what he saw happening in the vineyards of California.

The wines of a number of Golden State vineyards—small operations, with intriguing names and interesting stories—were finding a warm welcome among a growing population of upwardly mobile consumers increasingly interested in craft products. What Koch quickly found out was that many of these hot new vineyards were not real vineyards at all. They were marketing concepts: small, typically nonproducing vineyards that bought their wine from the larger vineyards and sold it with their own labels. While many did, indeed, offer excellent wines, their success was really the triumph of packaging and marketing; they delivered a quality product, yes, but what they were selling was a distinctive image to which a growing public responded. The strategy generated enormous enthusiasm for handcrafted California wines actually produced in mass-production vineyards.

It was a strategy that set Jim Koch's marketing antennas quivering. Typically in the beer business, the small brewers had tried to compete with the majors by cutting costs to offer cheaper beers. The obvious place to save money was in ingredients, but less expensive ingredients led to low-grade taste. A beer like Old Milwaukee was cheap enough, but no beer lover wanted to drink it more than once. Sacrificing quality therefore turned out to be an ill-conceived strategy. For those breweries that embraced the strategy, profits plummeted; all that was left was steadily increasing excess capacity.

What Koch concluded from all this was that the time and the market might be ripe for a craft beer, that Americans might be ready to embrace a beer with sophisticated taste and a handcrafted image, even—maybe especially—if the beer commanded a premium price. He came to another very important conclusion—that he could make a lot of this "handcrafted" beer very efficiently in an old brewery with excess capacity.

That is how Samuel Adams beer was first conceived, and it's the formula that made Jim Koch and his Boston Beer Company a smash hit in the new business of microbrewing. The concept was simple and brilliant: minimize your costs by finding a failing facility hungry enough for your business that it will charge you very little for turning out your quality product in quantity amounts, market the product aggressively, maximize profit margins. Contract brewing in a nutshell.

Jim actually found a number of regional breweries eager to become his contractor: from FX Matt Brewery in upstate New York, to the Old Lion in Pennsylvania, to Schmidt's Brewery in Minnesota. In the end, he reached an agreement with the Pittsburgh Brewing Company, and it was there that the Boston Beer Company got under way.

Of course, even for Jim Koch and the Boston Beer Company, the concept did not succeed overnight. It took a lot of hard work—as well as expert professional help. For the latter, Koch turned to Joe Owades, a well-known brewing consultant, who helped design Boston Beer's unique recipes. As to the hard work, that was mostly a matter of shoe leather. When Koch left his job at Boston Consulting, he brought with him his assistant, Rhonda Kallman, as sales manager for the new Boston Beer Company. The two proceeded to spend day and night pounding the pavement, trying to convince bar owners and storekeepers that Americans would pay premium prices for an American beer. Their selling of the company's signature Samuel Adams beer was a very personal, pioneering effort; they were up against a lot of skepticism. In fact, the local Boston beer distributors were so skeptical that Jim Koch bought a truck so he could distribute his beer himself. Eventually, of course, the effort paid off; Boston Beer Company became a great success, and both Jim and Rhonda have been reaping the rewards ever since.

In hindsight, of course, Koch's marketing instincts—and his timing—were outstanding. He was there just when word of mouth was spreading from the brew pubs of the Northwest to attract a similar consciousness in New England. The media was waking up to the microbrewing phenomenon, and Koch knew how to tell his story. Producing large volumes of craft beer at low cost for early and consistent profits formed a sound foundation for a scaleable business, and that's what Jim had built.

He had some good luck, too. As soon as the first kegs of Samuel Adams rolled off the production line, the beer was entered in the Great American Beer Festival, the annual competition in Denver, Colorado, that has since become a microbrewing shrine. It won the prestigious gold medal and gave birth to Koch's motto, "Best Beer in America." It also gave a great send-off to Samuel Adams, which became the first national microbrewing superstar. It still is the industry's biggest hit: Sam Adams sold more than 200,000 barrels by 1990, had U.S. sales equal to Heineken's by 1995, and was a public company with a market cap of $600 million by 1996.

Back in 1993, however, all Herm and I knew was that Jim Koch's Boston Beer Company model made a lot of sense. In my more sentimental moments, I suppose I would have preferred that we buy or build our own little brewery in a converted windmill on a canal. The reality, however, was that we simply had no choice but to go the route of contract brewing.

There was still another reason to go the contract route, and that reason, as Herm convinced me, was quality. From a brewer's point of view, the small, quaint breweries are not nearly as attractive as they seem to laymen. The large professional breweries are far better at achieving the high levels of sanitation control and consistency that make all the difference to the taste and quality of the beer. Popular though they might be among drinkers who like a touch of myth with their brew, most of the small breweries that had popped up were not making very good beer. Herm believed that what we really needed to make a high-quality, world-class beer was a high-quality, world-class brewery. We decided that we would look for one with excess capacity and the skills and standards to turn out our unique product under Herm's direction.

Our search was not as easy as it sounds. For one thing, we needed a particular piece of equipment, a yeast-measuring centrifuge found in very few breweries but essential to give *witbier* its characteristic cloudiness. We also needed to be able to bring in our own strain of yeast. Now yeasts are very frightening to brewers because one strain can easily contaminate another. That's the nature of yeast, of course, but such contamination will entirely change the nature of a particular brew. So we needed to find a brewery that would give us a separate yeast facility that only we would use.

By July, we had contacted five or six regional breweries that had the requisite excess capacity. Of these, only the Minnesota Brewing

Company in St. Paul had the centrifuge we needed. Fortunately, it was also big enough to give us a separate yeast facility. Most important, Minnesota Brewing was eager to do business with us. In its heyday, Minnesota had produced four million barrels of beer annually. Now production was down to about 300,000 barrels, and the company had only recently emerged from bankruptcy. The still-fretful owners of Minnesota Brewing were ready to deal. All that was left was to negotiate.

One of the things an entrepreneur needs is luck, although I tend to feel that the eager entrepreneur, by definition, is particularly open to luck. I had already had good luck in finding Herm Hegger. Now, another chance happening threw good fortune my way. Cravath had been retained to handle a very big public offering for a company based in St. Paul. I had been assigned to the case. The real windfall, however, was that the offices of Minnesota Brewing were just down the street from the company doing the securities offering. This meant that my travel to and accommodations in St. Paul were all courtesy of Cravath, Swaine & Moore's client. While I never stinted on work for the client, I also did not stint on my own work at the brewery. I remember one day when I taxied to the brewery for a six A.M. meeting, went into an all-day meeting with Cravath colleagues at nine, then dined with the brewery president that evening. I kept having to remind myself which identity I was about to assume—the solid corporate lawyer or the bold entrepreneur. Somehow I kept them straight and was able to get both jobs done. The result, as of July 1992, was that our fledgling beer company—already in possession of a recipe and a master brewer—had itself a brewery as well.

Now what we needed was about half a million dollars so we could actually start doing business.

6.

Starting a Business:

SEED WITH MONEY,
WATER WITH SKILLS

There are a number of paths to capital formation under U. S. laws, but at bottom, there's only one way to do it: you have to go out and ask people for money. That was the task I faced in the summer of 1992.

We had decided on a figure of $500,000 as seed money to get our operation going. Why $500,000? There was no particular magic to the amount; it just seemed like a logical, sensible kick-off price. Beer making does cost money. People insist on getting paid for their work. There are bills for everything from the ingredients of the brew to the energy that runs the brewing machinery. Half a million seemed like it would do the trick; it also struck me as an amount that would be possible to raise. Not easy, but possible.

The first thing I did was write a business plan and turn it into a private placement memo. "Private placement memo" is the legal term for a document that solicits financial backing for an enterprise from private individuals, offering them shares of ownership in the enterprise in return. The memo described the business proposition—the *witbier* phenomenon, the dimensions of the potential market, the progress to date, the prospects for the future—and told who I was and what I intended to do.

Preparing the private placement memo was an important exercise in its own right, for it forced me to put a value on the nascent company. It made me sit down and determine the number of shares I was going to sell and the number I would retain in what is called "founder's equity" or "sweat equity." I made the determinations pretty arbitrarily—I didn't know how else to make them; still don't— and arrived at the following calculations: I would contribute $75,000, my total savings, out of an initial capitalization of $500,000, and would retain 40 percent of the stock. The other 60 percent would be offered to investors.

With the valuation set and the private placement memo complete, I hit the streets to pitch the proposition to real-life backers. I first called on friends and family, but that produced only nominal success. Family finds it a bit difficult to take seriously a person they have chucked under the chin for nearly thirty years. Friends with whom you have spent Sunday mornings somehow cannot picture you as a CEO. None of this bothered me, for I sensed it would be better all around if I could raise the capital from third parties, serious investors whose approval, made manifest in cash, would validate the worth of my business proposition.

How did I find them? I simply asked everyone I knew if they knew someone who might be interested in investing in a beer company. An awful lot of people thought they did.

But when I got to these real-life potential backers, I quickly learned that no one was about to invest in a beer company without tasting the beer. That certainly made sense. On the other hand, it's pretty hard to give investors samples of a beer that you can't yet afford to brew, which is why you're looking for investors. Still, if I couldn't give people samples of our *witbier*, which had not yet been created, I could give them samples of generic *witbier*.

I flew back to Holland, drove to Herm's old brewery in Heumen, filled three large suitcases with six hundred bottles of *witbier*, stuffed two kegs of it into the trunk of the car, and headed back to the airport. I still have the photograph, taken by a friend, of me pushing a baggage cart loaded with this stuff into the departure building at

Schiphol Airport outside Amsterdam. I pushed the cart right up to the KLM check-in counter, where the clerk duly asked me what I had in the suitcases.

"Beer," said I.

"Oh?" said the KLM clerk. She eyed me warily.

"It's like this," I said, and I began to explain to her that my aged grandfather had grown up in the small town in Holland where the beer came from. My family, I went on, had asked me to bring this beer to the States as a present for the celebration next week of the old man's birthday, very possibly his last.

The clerk's wary look was transformed by this inspired fabrication into an almost misty-eyed smile. An equally mushy KLM manager spirited me and my luggage cart swiftly through the check-in process, waiving any charges for excess baggage. At JFK Airport in New York, more smiles greeted my story, which, by now, even I was beginning to believe. A bit misty-eyed myself, I lugged my beer freely if wearily through customs and into a taxi.

There I was, home at last, with six hundred bottles and two kegs of beer in the somewhat narrow kitchen of a Manhattan apartment.

My first move was to invest the two kegs in a beer-tasting party at a lively and well-known bar just a few blocks from my office. The idea was for people to taste the beer, like it, and spread the word among their friends. Not coincidentally, the guests were also people who could afford to invest, if convinced that Herm's beer was worth backing.

It was and they were. The kegs ran dry in no time. Some people wrote out checks on the spot. Others volunteered to introduce me to people they thought ought to know about this beer. Here at last was the confirmation we had been looking for—that New Yorkers loved *witbier* as much as Amsterdammers did.

In the weeks that followed, I used the six hundred bottles of *witbier* still in my kitchen sparingly, doling it out to prospective individual backers who could be convinced to give me twenty minutes to make my pitch. It was an arduous process. Each day, each meeting, seemed to present a new challenge—sometimes, a new obstacle. What I found interesting, however, was that I always came up with a response to the challenge, a burst of resourcefulness that surmounted the obstacle.

For example, how do you get chilled bottles of beer to potential backers when you're still spending ten-hour days as a Cravath lawyer?

I improvised, making use of what was at hand. And what is more "at hand" for a lawyer than the one essential that is an absolute mark of lawyerly identification? The litigation bag, of course. Wider and roomier than the normal briefcase or attaché, the litigation bag offered enough space for a small cooler. I kept a stash of Herm's beer in the office refrigerator, and when I had a meeting with a potential backer, I simply transferred a few bottles into the litigation bag cooler. Seeing me leave the office thus equipped, anyone from senior partner to nighttime cleaning staff would just assume that I was going out on business. Indeed I was, but much of the time, it was not Cravath, Swaine & Moore business.

I tried to arrange two or three meetings every day, usually in the late afternoon or evening—after all, I still owed the bulk of my time and energy to the people paying me. My secretary and a couple of close friends at work knew what I was really up to, but no one else at the firm was in on the secret. Fortunately, I'm a hard enough worker that my work at Cravath did not suffer.

Arduous as the process of winning backers was, however, it was also interesting and, very often, serendipitous.

There I would be, pitching my presentation and offering my samples, and most of the time people would listen politely and just as politely say no. On occasion, it's true, someone said yes. Between no and yes, however, there was often a different kind of response—a suggestion, an accidental encounter, a bit of luck.

There was the time, for example, when I was out making the fourth pitch of the day to a prospective investor who suddenly interrupted my rather hoarse presentation to ask who my accountants were.

I had to think fast. The truth was that we had no accountants as yet.

"Well," I stammered, "we, that is, there will be accountants at a certain point in time. That is, we will have financial statements that will be reported to investors, but we haven't really gotten that far yet."

"Uh huh," said my prospective investor, in whom I now had little hope. Then he said, "You may not be aware of this, but most of the Big Five accounting firms have what they call emerging business development capabilities that might be very useful to you." He went on to explain that the major accounting firms typically have little luck soliciting business from big corporate clients; rather, those firms already have their own accountants. Instead, the accounting firms systematically invest time and effort working with small businesses, helping them develop into bigger businesses and grateful clients. That means they may charge very little to do the accounting work of a young company or start-up venture in which they see potential.

This was welcome if astonishing news. I had simply assumed that the big accounting firms, like the big law firms, would have no interest in small businesses. But armed with my new information, I phoned a number of the Big Five firms and asked to speak to someone in the Emerging Business Development Group. Within a week, I had invitations to lunch from a series of accountants.

One of them, a partner with the prestigious Arthur Andersen, took me to lunch one day at one of the great French restaurants of New York, the sort of place I had first seen during my summer as a raw recruit being wined and dined by Simpson Thacher. "Well," he said, after we had ordered and the sommelier had opened and poured our bottle of wine, "what do you guess you'd be willing to pay in accounting fees for your first year?"

I looked around the restaurant at the investment bankers, corporate executives, and leisurely socialites lunching on grilled swordfish or cassoulet, saddle of lamb or an elegant soufflé. Probably about what you're going to pay for this lunch, I thought but did not say aloud. Instead I threw the question back to my lunch companion. "What do you think it would cost?" I asked.

He threw it right back to me. "What did you budget for accountants in your financial projections for the first year?"

I hurriedly tried to remember what number I had arbitrarily put down on the line for accounting services, and I couldn't, so I just as arbitrarily picked a number out of the air now. "I think we budgeted a thousand," I said.

"Fine," said the partner from Arthur Andersen. And that was how we got one of the top accounting firms on the planet to do all our financials and auditing for a thousand dollars a year for the first two years of our operation.

Of course, our "financials" at the time still consisted of my attempts to raise money from individual investors. As for our "operation," it was still just the recipe, Herm's expertise, and gearing up the brewery out in Minnesota. We still did not have a market positioning or even a very clearly defined marketing concept. That, too, was about to change—also as a result of a pitch to a prospective investor.

This time, the prospective investor was the friend of a friend of a friend—a corporate executive who reportedly liked beer. He liked *witbier* a lot, liked the business plan in my private placement memo, liked the whole venture enough to offer to invest $15,000. "By the way," he added as we wound up the meeting in his office over a cold *witbier* from my litigation bag, "you really ought to meet my cousin, John Mezzina."

John Mezzina was an advertising genius at Young & Rubicam, where he had been responsible for creating Joe Camel, the infamous but hugely effective cigarette advertising symbol. Mezzina and a colleague named Bill Brown had decided to leave Y&R to start up their own ad agency, Mezzina/Brown, and my newest investor thought they might like my beer, my story, and my proposed company. I took the phone number, called Mezzina, and arranged to have lunch the next day with him and Brown to try and sell the two of them on *witbier*.

I had scheduled an hour for the meeting; it went on all afternoon.

John and Bill and I hit it off fantastically. They immediately grasped the essence of what I was trying to do with *witbier* in America, and their creative juices began stirring like crazy, going to work at once on the all-important initial branding of our product. Name, logo, creative packaging, and a clearly focused marketing program: these were the critical ingredients, they convinced me, that could ensure *witbier*'s successful American launch. And they, Mezzina and Brown, were eager to pit their considerable talents and energies against the challenge.

Talent, energy, enthusiasm for *witbier*, and optimism for its success: it was a thrilling opportunity. The problem, again, was that the Douglas Beer Company had a very low budget; once again, I had the sorry feeling that the amount set aside for agency fees in the business plan just about equaled the tab for our lunch.

To this concern, John and Bill offered an irresistible solution: they agreed to create a brand identity and do all the creative work for the company in exchange for stock. We agreed in principle to proceed on this equity basis, and we scheduled a meeting for the following evening, along with their legal counsel and financial advisor, to craft the details of the agreement.

The following evening, I showed up at Mezzina/Brown headquarters with my private placement memorandum, a calculator, copies of my contracts with Herm and Minnesota Brewing, and a briefcase full of cold *witbiers*. Goodwill abounded, but the agreement itself seemed headed toward an impassable divide.

I had asked John and Bill to price the value of their services in dollar terms and then to accept payment in common stock priced at the same price that the other private placement investors were accepting. While both men agreed that this was both logical and fair, the sum total of shares that they would thus acquire seemed to them insufficient return on all the hard work they and their staff would have to contribute to do the job right. They simply wanted to own more of the company if they were going to throw themselves into making it a big success.

On the other hand, I argued that it would be impossible to attract additional investors if we had to disclose that such a large percentage of our operating budget was going into the creation of marketing materials and packaging design—especially since my initial plan had promised that *witbier* would succeed by its genuine appeal and word of mouth, as other microbrews had.

Just when it seemed we might never find a solution, Bill dropped a suggestion into the gap that in a million years I never would have dreamed of. What if, he said, Mezzina/Brown contributed $100,000 in cash to the new company? Then they could own as much as 10 percent of it.

The deal was done within minutes. And I could hardly contain my excitement.

A few days later, more good luck came my way—this time from a fellow who offered neither investment money nor any special service, just invaluable advice. The fellow was Terry Liebman, whose family had operated the now-defunct Rheingold Brewery. The Liebmans had sold the Rheingold brand rights to the Stroh Company long ago, before the decline of local and regional breweries, and now Terry wanted to buy back the rights and reestablish Rheingold as a microbrew. Obviously, Terry was not about to invest in our microbrew, but he was generous enough to offer the following recommendation:

"Before you do another thing," Terry counseled, "call a guy named Joe Owades."

I've mentioned Joe Owades before, as the consultant who helped Jim Koch create the recipes for Samuel Adams beers. In fact, Owades is a legend in the annals of brewing. A brewmaster with a Ph.D. in yeast biology, Joe had worked at Anheuser-Busch, Carling, and a number of other major breweries. He had also worked for the Liebmans at Rheingold, where he had actually invented the world's first light beer. At the time, Rheingold made the decision to market the product as a diet beer—a disastrous decision, as it turned out, resulting in total failure. A year or so later, however, the Miller Brewing Company copied the process Joe had invented and positioned the product as a "less filling" alternative. The whole category of light beer took off running after that, and it hasn't stopped since.

By that time, however, Joe had left the big brewing environment. With the emergence of microbreweries in the late 1970s and early 1980s, he turned his hand to consulting and quickly became the most successful, most sought after, and most highly listened-to voice in the business. He was responsible for the beers brewed by Anchor Steam and Pete's Wicked, to name just a couple, not to mention the Sam Adams beers of the Boston Beer Company.

Terry not only suggested I try to hire Joe, he also gave me an introduction. Without that, Joe would almost surely not have agreed to see me. Even with the introduction, I was in for a bumpy ride—and I don't mean the flight to San Francisco or the drive up to Joe's home in the Sonoma wine country. Owades may live in the laid-back, mellow precincts of northern California, but he was born in Brooklyn and does not suffer fools gladly. I had brought along a cold six-pack of Herm's *witbier* from Holland for Joe to taste, and he was not shy about expressing his reaction.

Joe sipped the beer, stared at it, smelled it, tested it with litmus papers, and sipped it again. "It's not fucking beer," he declared. For all his training and studying, Joe Owades had never seen a Belgian *witbier* and had certainly never tasted one. To be sure, he was fascinated by the story of the *witbier* phenomenon, but he was also skeptical—unsure that the cloudy texture was anything more than a breakdown in the brewing process, incredulous that anyone would want to drink such a cloudy brew. In the end, I think more out of curiosity than out of any belief in our future success, he agreed to work for us. What's more, he agreed to accept half his normal consulting fee, and to accept stock.

On the trip back to New York, I could not help but feel excited about all the progress made to date. Douglas Beer Company had not yet closed its financing or hired its first full-time employee, but it had a world-class team aboard: an authentic Belgian master brewer, the industry's top brewing consultant, a Big Five accounting firm, and one of the hottest young advertising shops on or off Madison Avenue. I couldn't have been happier. It is hard enough to hire the best talent when you can afford it. In this case, however, the best talent had been inspired not only to join my venture but, in effect, to invest in it. They believed in it enough to be willing to risk for it; they made that clear by putting their considerable skills, their energy, and their resources on the line. I could not have asked for more or better.

To top it all off, all of this new talent gave an air of credibility to the Douglas Beer Company as it pursued its first financing. And by December of 1992, I had managed to raise the $500,000 we had targeted—enough money, finally, to produce a first run of beer.

It was an exciting moment, but it was also a wake-up call. No more homework. No more dress rehearsal. The meter was running—on other people's money! It was time to quit the law firm and launch a beer company. I chose the day of Cravath's annual Christmas bash to announce that I was resigning at the end of the year.

To my astonishment, my announcement angered no one. On the contrary. While I think—and hope—that Cravath senior management was sorry to lose someone they thought of as a valuable employee, even the most aloof partners were full of good wishes for my future. Starting a beer company, an outlandish proposition, seemed to tickle the imagination of many a hardworking corporate lawyer. In fact, one of the senior partners popped into my office the next day to ask if I were interested in raising more capital.

I stayed up late that night writing a second private placement memorandum, which I handed to him in the morning. That's when I learned about an interesting Cravath policy I would never otherwise have been privy to. Before any Cravath partner invests in a private company, he or she, as a matter of courtesy, shares the opportunity with all the partners. The *witbier* opportunity was shared at the weekly partners' lunch that very afternoon. By the next morning, no fewer than twenty Cravath partners had requested copies of the second memorandum, and by the end of the following day, I had signed subscriptions from fourteen of my soon-to-be-former employers. In fact, the offering, for $300,000, was oversubscribed. Seemingly awash in cash, I happily returned the balance of funds and closed the transaction by allocating each subscribing partner only a portion of the amounts offered.

A week after my resignation, Liesbeth and I enjoyed a keyed-up, expectant New Year's Eve. When I woke up the morning of January 1, 1993, it really was the first day of the rest of my life. I had embarked on something completely new—not just new for me, but new for the business world as well. It hadn't been done before. Maybe that's what made it so exciting.

7.

Free to Ferment

The first challenge was operational. We needed an office, a staff, a distribution network. Not to mention a name for the beer, a bottle and six-pack design, and a sales and marketing plan.

With all this on the to-do list, it seemed a sensible first move to hire at least one employee. Tim Klem, the brother-in-law of a friend of mine, had submitted his résumé a few weeks before Christmas. A recent Yale graduate with a perfect grade-point average, Tim sure looked good on paper. He made an even better impression in person. We met in the lobby of my apartment building, and that's where I hired him. He started work immediately.

We made our first decision at once; we determined to base our operation in the Soho district in downtown Manhattan. The reason was partly selfish: I lived only a few blocks away and looked forward to commuting on foot. But Soho was also the right location for what we were trying to accomplish.

Famous for its cast-iron architecture, the Soho district had originally been built for industry, but as industry faded from Manhattan in the 1950s and 1960s, artists began occupying the vast loft spaces. After the artists came the galleries, then the restaurants, then the trendy shops. Today, Soho is the nerve center of everything that is "downtown"—forward-thinking and pace-setting in art, music, theater, and fashion. We wanted our beer to belong there.

But when we started, we were hardly on the cutting edge of chic. Our office, on the corner of Spring and Lafayette Streets, was no more than 200 square feet with a tiny window in the back and chipping paint on the walls. But the rent was cheap—dirt cheap for Manhattan—and the landlord was "flexible," two important factors for a business that expected rapid expansion but wasn't quite sure when it would start.

Into the global headquarters of what was now known as the Spring Street Brewing Company, we moved and furnished it with second-hand metal desks, foldaway office chairs, and a refrigerator jammed with beer. We bought two slightly out-of-date computers, a decent printer, a fax machine, and a large black filing cabinet. From this hub of operations, we set out to conquer the world of beer.

It was a two-pronged effort. Out in Minnesota, Herm and Joe Owades were focused on brewing our beer. To stay on top of developments on that front, I shuttled frequently between New York and St. Paul. Back in New York, the top priority was positioning the product the master brewers were working on. Here my mentors were John Mezzina and Bill Brown, master brewers in their own right, except that what they were brewing up was a brand identity.

It was an exciting process—creative and fun. To probe the market, we instituted some fairly unusual focus group interviews. Basically, what we did was go to a bar and ask the assembled beer drinkers to react to different prototypes for labels and logos, and to respond to different suggested beer names. This taught us what would not work.

The name Mezzina and Brown came up with, Wit, was, in my view, exactly right. Simple and distinctive, it sounded both foreign and familiar, and it had the great advantage of being absolutely descriptive of the product and playfully punning at the same time. But if the Mezzina/Brown idea for the name was perfect, their vision of it was absolutely spectacular. *WIT!* it proclaimed, the word topping a vivid exclamation point to create a logo that was unique and unforgettable. When we had all agreed on this basic look, John and Bill went to work to create the marketing campaign.

Meanwhile, the first batch of beer out of the barrel in St. Paul was not quite right. It was necessary to try again. Herm and Joe hunkered down at the brewery, and I flew back to New York to take the next step—finding a wholesaler.

The first thing anyone in the beer business has to learn is that there is an absolutely essential middleman between the brewery producing beer and the retail stores, restaurants, and bars distributing it. That is the wholesaler, and no beer company can function without him.

There are four major wholesalers in New York City, where we had decided to launch Wit. I made appointments to see all four. Since we still had no beer from our own brewery, I took bottles of Herm's beer and sanded off the crown of the bottle, the part that had his logo on it. Armed with these samples and a notebook full of prototype material from Mezzina/Brown, I went off to do battle with the all-powerful wholesalers.

Whether it was the uniqueness of the brew, the artwork we were able to show them, or a combination of the two, all four wholesalers expressed interest in carrying Wit. Since we had our pick, we chose the top of the crop, the biggest in the city. The wholesaler for Corona, Rolling Rock, and Samuel Adams would now be carrying Wit as well.

It was the beginning of March. Spring was just around the corner. We expected to launch Wit in May. It seemed a good idea to do some advance work—to try to sell the beer to bars and restaurants so it would be in stock when the Wit bandwagon started rolling and, we hoped, upped the demand. Tim and I sanded all the crowns off the remaining bottles of beer from Herm's brewery, bought a bunch of small, portable coolers, and put together two display books of labels. We were ready. "Wear a suit tomorrow," I admonished Tim as we closed up the office the night before our planned assault on the city's bars. Tim nodded.

The next day, disguised as stockbrokers in three-piece suits, ties, and wingtips, Tim and I set out to brave the elements. The elements, as it turned out, had a big surprise for us. It may have said "spring" on the calendar, but Nature had decided to let loose one last blizzard for the winter of 1992–93, and it chose that precise day to do it. We single-mindedly kept slogging through drifts that were bringing the city to a halt, trudging from bar to restaurant to bar to make our presentations. Whether it was our fortitude, the peculiar sight of two guys in suits selling beer in a blizzard, or Wit itself, I still can't be sure, but the response was tremendous, as bar after bar signed up to carry Wit.

We did the same thing on the following day—with new shoes this time, having ruined the first pair in the blizzard. We ruined this pair, too, but we signed up a lot more bars. By day three, we had decided to wear snow boots and, to complete the picture, casual clothing. We sold so much beer this day that we decided we never had to wear suits again—another indication, if one were needed, that we had chosen the right profession.

Day after day for a month and a half, Tim and I in person introduced Wit to bars and restaurants around the city and in the Hamptons of eastern Long Island. By May, more than three hundred establishments had signed up to carry our beer.

We also had a plan to drum up more excitement about the launch of the beer by getting cafés around town to sport Wit umbrellas. A lot of beer companies, we learned, gave out café umbrellas, but none of them provided umbrella stands. Tim and I decided to make stands to go with our umbrellas. On a Friday night, we drove out to a huge Home Depot in New Jersey, bought hundreds of small plastic buckets, bags of cement, PCV tubing, and masking tape, and brought it all back to the office. The next morning, we begged the use of the hose from the building's landlord, mixed cement, cut the PCV tubing into two-foot-long pipes, and, with Liesbeth's help, spent the day making little cement-filled buckets with tubes sticking up from the middle of them. The result may have been the work of amateurs, but it worked. By the time we were ready to launch Wit, some two hundred of our umbrellas were planted in stands at cafés all over town.

The official launch date was Memorial Day of 1993, the idea being to pitch Wit initially as a new summer drink—perfect for city or beach. The night before the launch, we threw a press party at a New York bar called Mr. Fuji Tropicana. That worked, too. During week one of the Wit launch, the Wit story was reported in *New York* magazine, local television news, and the daily press. CNN covered us, too, and the *Wall Street Journal* ran a piece about the involvement of Mezzina/Brown.

More bars kept signing up—by August, Wit was available in more than four hundred establishments—and everywhere you looked that summer in New York, people seemed to be seeing, hearing about, or drinking Wit Beer. The broad exposure reached to other regions. Wholesalers from cities all over the United States started calling, inviting us to start selling in their regions. Impressed by our publicity and our initial success, they wanted us to export both to their neck of the woods. Clearly, ours had been a highly successful launch. Thanks to the committed hard work of a handful of us, not to mention the backing from our investors, we had shot out of the starting gate like champions.

But just as we were coming up on the first turn, we began to see how arduous the course could be, how difficult the track conditions. We had done everything right. Better than right: we had been creative, effective, and smashingly successful. But it was becoming clear that the beer business was a highly competitive one and, as a small company with limited resources, that we faced a Herculean task. Our biggest competitor in the microbrew category, for example, was Samuel Adams, which boasted a sales force of sixty-seven people— five of them in New York alone. By contrast, Wit had a sales force of two, who also served as the business managers, accountants, quality controllers, public relations gurus, and all-around chief cooks and bottle washers. Even with charm, personality, and a fantastic product, we were hardly a match for the superior forces ranged against us.

Beyond being outnumbered and outprovisioned, we could see we were in for a tough fight. Competition in the beer business, we learned, is no-holds-barred. Bigger, better-equipped competitors stampeded the store owners who had given us a prominent exhibit and plenty of shelf space; a point-of-sale display we put up on Monday was often down by Tuesday. We also found that the bars and restaurants that had been eager to try something new were not particularly good at sustaining the initial burst of activity; they just waited for the next new thing to come along.

Everyone agreed we had a good product. And everyone thought we were a good small company that had made a very good beginning. We needed to capitalize on those strengths if we were going to grow into a bigger company with staying power. Marketing and sales were the key. "You need to educate people about Wit," bar owners and restaurateurs would tell us. "When are you going to do more advertising?" the store owners demanded to know.

It was becoming evident that the money I had raised to seed the Wit launch wasn't nearly enough for a meaningful, effective sales and marketing operation. In fact, we were losing about $20,000 a month in the effort to introduce Wit. That's not unusual for a start-up venture, but clearly, the hemorrhaging of cash could not continue indefinitely. We needed a transfusion. It was up to me to raise more money.

8.

Some Capital Ideas

Where do you look? Where does a small, start-up venture go to find capital? I believed that we needed about $2 million—maybe $3 million—to get Spring Street Brewing Company and Wit to the next level of competitive capability. I had already gone the route of applying to friends and family and of pounding the pavements to make one-on-one appeals to friends of friends and family. I felt I could not keep dipping in these same wells. What's more, I didn't think I could obtain access to enough such individuals with enough money to raise the amount we needed.

The obvious first step was to the venture capitalists. Venture capital companies, after all, exist to make money available for investment in new, young, innovative enterprises. It seemed to me that Spring Street Brewing Company certainly qualified. So I prepared a presentation and began soliciting meetings with venture capitalists. Based on the media exposure, with its reports on the quality of our product and our packaging, this effort met with considerable response. Lots of venture capitalists were eager to do a lot of listening, but talking to them turned out to be a laborious, time-consuming, and ultimately futile process.

Perhaps not surprisingly, there is a rigid hierarchy at work in most venture capital firms—a filter system that no doubt helps sift the crashworthy from the cashworthy in a way that's efficient for the venture capital firms themselves. It's highly inefficient, however, for the young entrepreneur.

First, I would meet with some very junior people who listened to the presentation and then critiqued the business plan. "We're interested," they would say, "but we need you to prepare this projection or that forecast. Do all that, then come back and see us." So I would do all that—which invariably meant a great deal of hard work—and then I would be invited back to meet with some mid-level people on the next higher rung of the hierarchy. And they would also tell me what an interesting little company I had, but before any decision could be made, they would really need to see this analysis or that estimate. Back I would go to my humble office, where I would burn the midnight oil preparing all the information these guys had demanded, in exactly the format they wanted, complying to the letter with their every request. Then I would return for meeting number three, only to learn that nobody I had been speaking to had any authority to make any decision at all, that I was still a long way from anyone who did, and that I had to do yet more homework.

For nearly six months, I worked very hard trying to attract sophisticated institutional venture capital. All along the way, the feedback was very positive; in fact, in many respects, the process was both flattering and encouraging. It was also exasperating; while the compliments were coming in, the money was going out. We were simply going to have to find some alternative other than the venture capitalists.

In the meantime, however, our treasury was down to about $100,000. To fill the corporate coffers, a stopgap measure was needed. There was no choice but to look for more individual investors. While Spring Street Brewing could show only modest sales and a monthly loss that would continue to eat away at capital for a while, we could at least demonstrate that we had created something real, we had done something substantial, and we had a product that was in many ways highly successful. That meant we could ask investors for a higher per-share price than was paid by those original investors who had backed me on nothing more than a bottle of Herm's beer and the couple of contracts I had engineered. I split the common stock of the company, tripled the stock price, and wrote a third private placement memorandum seeking $2 million in investment. Then I hit the road to make my pitch to anyone who would listen.

Even finding listeners proved tough this go-round, not to mention getting inside to make my pitch or convincing them to put up money. To get some ideas, I called on a number of beer distributors flush with cash from the high margins they were making on all that micro-brewed beer. I visited every investor from the first round of private placements, asking them for the names of colleagues and associates.

I chased leads from coast to coast. Sometimes it felt like I was chasing air.

In Washington, D.C., I met the parents of one of our new employees, who promised to show my private placement to Bill Gates. We filled a box with T-shirts, Wit caps, a six-pack, and an original draft beer tap handle, and shipped it off to the Microsoft campus. Excited and optimistic, I then flew across the country for the expected meeting with the richest man in the world—only to learn on arrival that Gates's personal financial officer had decided "not to pursue the opportunity."

Another Seattle contact, however, who didn't want me to go home empty-handed, set up a meeting with another billionaire, Bruce McCaw, brother of Steve and part owner of the McCaw Cellular telephone empire. McCaw allotted me forty-five minutes of his time. He spent forty of them showing me models of NASCAR racers he sponsored and urging that Spring Street should also sponsor a car. Who was pitching whom?

Back in New York, I managed to meet an heir to the Sears, Roebuck fortune, a friendly and long-established venture capitalist. I had four meetings with him, getting as far as the serious due diligence phase, but the verdict was still a vote against Spring Street and Wit Beer.

I also met someone who said he could get me in to see John Reed, the president of Citibank. Again I packed an impressive box of Wit goodies and had it hand-delivered to the bank's executive headquarters on Park Avenue. I followed up with phone calls to Reed's office. Lots of phone calls. One a day for a week at least. I did not reach Reed, or Reed's secretary, or Reed's secretary's assistant. I did manage to leave a message for the assistant, however, and three weeks later I got a call telling me that the package had been received and that Mr. Reed would be in touch if he had any interest. Apparently, he did not.

So it went for the better part of three months. I was persistent. I had faith. I maintained an optimistic outlook, the expectation that the big backer was only one more call away. Such an attitude is essential, I think, when you're in the position I was in. You need the confidence of a struggling actor going to his next audition just to get out the door to make your pitch each day.

But at the end of the process, I had managed to raise only $400,000—a long way from the hoped-for $2 million and not a great vote of confidence in Wit. For the six people now employed at Spring Street Brewing, I tried to put the best possible spin on what was, realistically, a pretty dire financial situation. True, I said, $400,000 is only a small percentage of the wherewithal we need to grow and flourish. On the other hand, it ain't chicken feed; it will give us a breathing space, room to maneuver.

And maneuver we did. I returned to focusing full-time on beer. We added some wholesalers, entered a few more states, began to see some real growth. Sales doubled in our second year, and our return on expense, although still negative, improved markedly. In our first year, we had spent $2.40 to market every $1 worth of beer. The next year, we whittled that down to less than $1.75 per $1 of beer, and we were on track to cut that figure down to breakeven—a dollar spent for a dollar earned—by year three. We were not yet profitable, but our numbers were moving in the right direction.

To keep them moving that way, we introduced a second product: Amber Wit. Still a wheat beer, the Amber Wit is darker and more full-bodied than *witbier*. It is spiced with cumin, giving it a different taste, and it is an uncloudy beer. But it was a logical extension of our product line: where the original Wit had been marketed as a refreshing summer drink, Amber Wit was positioned as a richer, more muscular cold-weather brew. The time was right to add a product. The more products you have available, the more you can sell.

And we were selling more. Amber Wit was launched to strong reviews and wide on-premise consumer acceptance. It sold well and helped us sell more of the original Wit into the bargain. But we still faced the same problem we had confronted from day one: we weren't making any money. Our competition remained so outsized that our growth made barely a dent. We had no real marketing budget. No advertising budget. Our way of doing business was to go door to door, signing up another bar here, another restaurant there. It was picturesque, but there was no way it could spark the growth we were looking for. Soon enough, our cash flow again needed radical attention. With only $200,000 left in the till, I was once more facing the challenge that had been breathing down the neck of the Wit enterprise from the very beginning: raising money so we could grow.

To rev up my creative motor, I sat down with Mark Morrisey and Richard Wise, two of the senior marketing gurus at Mezzina/Brown. Over the course of two weeks, we worked out an absolutely world-class marketing and advertising plan. Not a single detail was overlooked—from the cost of outdoor billboards in Atlanta to the insertion schedules for every alternative city newspaper from Manhattan to San Francisco.

To execute the plan, Mezzina/Brown unleashed the full talents of its creative team under the leadership of the awesome Dinius Jaras, the original creator of Wit's graphic identity. Over the next weeks, we created package designs for an entire line of seasonal Wit products. We made a stunning design for a bold, colorful Wit can. And we produced a full line of advertising and promotional materials that could easily compete with the stuff coming out of the largest microbreweries—dartboards, running wear, ashtrays, even fancy neckties.

All we needed now was the cash to bankroll the production of these materials and the implementation of our fabulous plan.

I went back to the venture capitalists. They were encouraging and enthusiastic, clearly impressed with the scope of our plans and quite dazzled with the quality of the Mezzina/Brown work. As before, they were interested in where we were and encouraged by how it was going, and as before, none of them gave us a dime. In fact, most raised the bar over the last time I had been in to see them, setting higher and higher thresholds we would have to attain before they could "commit." Be patient, they seemed to be telling us; take more time to grow, and it will require less money. But given the nature of our business and the industry's competitive pressures, we simply didn't have the time.

I reassessed the situation. It was now the autumn of 1994. We had been in business a little over two years. We had a terrific plan and all the creative material with which to execute it. We were definitely on a growth path. We were winning awards at beer festivals. People clearly liked Wit and Amber Wit. They wrote us letters about how much they liked it. They telephoned to ask where they could find it. Lots of people. Thousands of them.

Was that it? Was that the solution? What if we could turn those thousands of Wit Beer lovers into Wit shareholders? Would that do it?

I was suddenly reminded of an experience that belonged to my college days in the Boston area in the early 1980s. This fantastic new specialty ice cream had come to town, and I was crazy about it. So were thousands of my fellow students, professors, bank clerks, Boston Brahmins, politicians, street cleaners, and no doubt the entire rosters of the Boston Red Sox, Celtics, and Bruins. Our devotion to this ice cream proved to have far-reaching consequences, thanks to the clever thinking on the part of the two guys who owned the ice cream company.

The guys were Ben Cohen and Jerry Greenfield. Back in 1978, these two friends-since-childhood had each put up $4,000, then together borrowed another $4,000 to start an ice cream company in a renovated gas station in Burlington, Vermont. Their recipe for success was to use fresh Vermont milk and cream and introduce innovative flavors—and to let everyone know about both aspects of their product. In just a few years, Ben & Jerry's became a highly successful company with a very popular product, but they were still only a regional operation, and they remained a very small operation.

In the early 1980s, Cohen and Greenfield had the idea to raise money by selling their stock to their customers. Nothing could be better, they believed, than having the people who buy your product also own your company. You not only raise money; you also raise the level of support on the part of your customers, so that those customers talk up your product to their friends and relatives, who also become customers—and maybe also shareholders.

What made this wonderful idea particularly brilliant was the way Cohen and Greenfield marketed ownership in their company: they decorated their ice cream cartons with announcements inviting customers to scoop up shares of Ben & Jerry's stock. That was what I was now remembering, as I pondered how to move Spring Street Brewing to the next upward level of growth: the sight of the stock offering prospectus on the half-pint carton that was my almost daily ice cream fix when I was in college. Had I had any money to spare back then, I would not have hesitated to invest it in Ben & Jerry's ice cream.

In fact Ben and Jerry had reserved stock exclusively for their customers. The results were just what they had intended: a new level of customer loyalty and enough money to grow into the nationwide titan they are today.

If Ben & Jerry could raise money from their ice cream eaters, why couldn't Spring Street Brewing Company raise money from its beer drinkers? We knew there were a lot of people out there who thought Wit was terrific and believed the enterprise had considerable potential. Could we not turn this following into an army of investors who would signal their support with their capital and at the same time be boosters for Wit products, pestering their local bars and supermarkets to stock our beer?

That was the germ of the idea that would change the way we raised money and, eventually, spark a revolution in securities trading.

At that moment, though, the idea was a simple response to an immediate need: If we could get ourselves in a position to sell stock directly to the public legally, the public would buy it. At least, that was
what I was betting on. The next step, therefore, was to find the right
way to sell the stock.

Under the securities laws in this country, you can sell stock in one
of two ways. You can either solicit the public in general or sell to private buyers in particular. The first way, the public way, means
that you're offering stock to people you don't know and who don't
know you. They don't know a lot about your company's financial affairs, and you don't know a lot about theirs. That is why the public offering is governed by stringent registration rules on both the federal
and state levels. The rules require you to create and file with the appropriate government agency a detailed prospectus. The prospectus
is subject to scrutiny and comments about the level and quality of
your disclosure. Unless and until the government is satisfied that you
have disclosed all the material facts about your company clearly and
intelligently, you cannot actually sell the stock. But once you have
cleared this registration process, you are free to make a public offering of shares of stock in your company; it is considered then that the
public has access to all the information it needs to make an informed
decision about your stock.

If you don't want to go through all that disclosure and registration
and waiting time, you're left with the other way of selling stock, the
private way. In a private placement, by definition, you may not solicit
the general public. You may not advertise, send a mailing, broadcast
on radio or television. In fact, you must limit a private placement to
accredited investors, or angel investors as they are sometimes called.
Accredited investors are wealthy people—individuals with a million
dollars of net worth or who draw down over $200,000 per year in in-
come. The law considers them sufficiently sophisticated financially
that they can understand the risks of investing; they don't need the
protection of the registration process and of government scrutiny.
That imposes a certain limitation on the company issuing stock—i.e.,

while you don't have to go through a lengthy registration process, you cannot just solicit anyone. Only rich anyones. What's more, in a private placement, the stock can only be traded privately. It remains illiquid for at least a year after the private placement; that is, it cannot be traded in a public market during that time.

Small, early-stage companies like Spring Street generally do not contemplate selling stock to the public. One reason is that the registration process itself is both expensive and time-consuming, and few developing enterprises can afford to expend either the financial or the human resources.

Another reason small companies traditionally do not sell their shares in public offerings is more subtle, but perhaps more important. Conventional wisdom says that public investors will only buy shares in public offerings if, after the offering, those shares become liquid—tradable on listed exchanges or through the NASDAQ stock market.

But stock in small companies typically does not become liquid; it does not get listed on an exchange. Why? The answer lies in the way the capital markets work:

For one thing, only large companies tend to be able to meet the listing requirements of the large stock exchanges. Smaller companies can be traded over-the-counter on NASDAQ, but only if securities firms, called market makers, are willing to put their capital at risk to buy and sell shares in a small company's stock—make a market in the stock—to ensure liquidity. In addition, the securities firms must provide research coverage so that investors will want to invest in the stock.

Not surprisingly, the major investment banks tend not to bother underwriting the issues of small companies. They prefer to focus on less risky, more developed enterprises, enterprises with fairly deep management teams, enterprises that have demonstrated stable revenue growth and some profits as well. In fact, most investment banks won't touch a financing that seeks less than $15 million. Spring Street Brewing didn't qualify on any one of these criteria: we weren't large enough or stable enough or seeking enough capital to attract an investment bank—at least, an investment bank with any kind of reputation.

I believed, nevertheless, that there were people who would be willing to buy shares in Spring Street in a public offering despite the fact that there was no immediate expectation of liquidity, and even though there was no investment bank in the deal, no research, and no market-making support. These public investors, I believed, would be just as patient as the typical private placement investors. The combination of their public offering–style investment and their private-placement–style patience would give us both the capital and the time we needed to develop further, to grow enough, so that later on we could spark the interest of major investment banks, market makers, and research analysts.

To make it happen, I set out to do something unprecedented, as far as I could determine, in the annals of investing, something new altogether. I crafted a hybrid—part public offering, part private placement. I devised a kind of stock that complied with the registration rules and therefore could be sold publicly, but at the same time remained an illiquid issue that would not be traded in the public market. This offered the best of both worlds: by complying with the registration process we were in a position to direct our offering to public investors, to Wit enthusiasts, true believers in our product, willing and able to buy small, long-term shares in our future; but still, because our stock would remain illiquid, we would be free of the pressures that come with being a publicly traded company.

What this hybrid in effect said to investors was this: Look, folks, we're going through the registration process for your protection—something to which every potential investor is entitled—but you should understand that the stock is not going to be liquid. At least, not for a good while. The registration process means that we can legally sell the stock and you can legally buy it, but you need to think of this stock as a long-term investment. In contrast to a traditional public offering, you won't be able to trade it on a national market anytime soon. This is like venture capital. This is like the stock that accredited investors buy in private placements. All we're doing is breaking it up into smaller units.

On the other hand, you're getting in on the ground floor of an opportunity that usually is open only to rich people and institutional investors.

That was the gist of the offering I wanted to make. To do so, I had to register it with the Securities and Exchange Commission at the federal level and with the appropriate agencies of whatever individual states I thought should carry the offering.

Spring Street had one very important advantage as far as launching the registration process was concerned: my background as a securities lawyer. If we had had to go out and hire me, it would have cost at least $50,000. In fact, companies that hire a Cravath-class lawyer to write a prospectus and guide them through the arcana of the Securities and Exchange Commission can easily see their bills climb to $200,000.

So I set about preparing the SEC registration, and at the same time I reviewed the so-called Blue Sky laws of individual states. Blue Sky laws are said to have gotten their name when a judge ruled that a particular stock being offered had "about the same value as a patch of blue sky." In short, the Blue Sky laws have been enacted at the state level to protect the public against securities fraud. Before a stock can be sold in a state, you need to go through a state registration process in addition to the SEC registration. And like the SEC process, state registration requires full disclosure of all aspects of the investment.

Some states make it easier than others. New York, for example, lets you sell just about anything to just about anybody. That was good, because New York was one of the states I had targeted—states with the strongest Wit markets. Other target states, however, proved to be literally inaccessible. California, for one, still feeling the sting of a legacy of penny-stock frauds, categorically bans any stock offering priced lower than $2 per share. Since we had again split out stock and were now planning to issue shares of Wit at $1.85, California was a no go. In Massachusetts and Minnesota, we encountered stiff resistance to offerings from any small company that had not yet shown a profit and compiled a long operating history. While neither state said no, their requests for compliance proved so onerous, so harshly demanding, that I opted to cut our losses.

Then there was Florida, which charges $2,000 just to register a small stock offering, and then takes about a year before it renders its approval. Not good for a bleeding company seeking a cash transfusion. Meanwhile, Texas, New Jersey, and a few other states required me to pass lengthy exams before I could qualify as Spring Street's authorized stock salesman. I crammed hard and passed the exams.

Inch by inch, we were coming to the edge of the legal forest. In the meantime, we had been working full out on a marketing plan, a way to get the public's attention and sell our stock, in much the same way as we sold them our beer. First, we printed an announcement about the stock offering on our labels, proclaiming our toll-free 800 number and promising every caller a prospectus on the offering. Then we created a range of marketing materials with the 800 number—posters, postcards, bottleneck ringers, all sorts of things. The plan was to distribute these materials in bars and restaurants and at beer festivals—anywhere beer drinkers congregate—advising them about the offering and urging them to call.

Of course, each toll-free call from our potential investors would cost us about 35 cents. The marketing materials cost in the tens of thousands of dollars. The whole situation was beginning to be a genuine catch-22: we needed to raise money so we could make money, and we needed to spend money in order to raise money. With capital down to some $200,000, I did something I really had not wanted to do: I went back to a dozen or so wealthy friends of Wit. This time, I made them a preferred-stock offer they couldn't refuse: If they purchased shares of a special preferred stock I created, and if our public offering raised a million dollars or more within six months, then they would double their money. We would pay them twice the face value of the preferred stock in cash. If we failed to raise the million in six months, however, the investors could convert their preferred stock into common stock at a conversion ratio that represented a common stock price of 30 cents a share—a huge discount off the $1.85-per-share price we were charging in the public offering.

Fortunately, this eleventh-hour desperation move worked. In only a few days, I was able to raise $250,000, the bridge financing we needed if we were going to market our offering in earnest. We just had to get enough posters and ringers and six-packs to enough people, so that enough of them would call and ask for the prospectus, so that enough of those people would invest enough money in Wit Beer. The challenge was really to get the word out.

Finally, after a number of halts, retreats, and reassessments, we filed with the securities commissions in twenty-two states and registered Wit stock so we could be in a position to sell it to the public.

The next morning, I put out a subdued press release that announced the essential facts: A microbrewery, Spring Street Brewing, was taking itself public. It was seeking to raise up to $5 million, offering 2.8 million shares at $1.85 per share in an initial public offering. It was setting up an 800 number for prospective investors. Period, paragraph, end of press release. The terseness was deliberate; the registration process was under way, and we were in what is called the quiet period, which meant we were strictly limited as to what we could say or claim about our company or our offering.

To my delight, the Reuters wire service picked up the press release, and *USA Today* ran a 4-inch news story that included a photo of Wit Beer and the toll-free 800 number.

Wow.

By week's end, we had received more than six thousand phone calls on the 800 number from people expressing interest and requesting a prospectus. Tim, Liesbeth, and I were glued to our phones from dawn to midnight for the better part of a week. Even that wasn't enough. Every time one of us hung up a phone, the voice-mail system registered another thirty messages.

One of the messages was from the local Fox TV news show, inviting me to appear on the broadcast to talk about the offering. The invitation sparked quite a debate between Andy, the putative beer magnate, and Klein, the former lawyer. Klein reminded Andy that anything said during the quiet period might be considered part of the prospectus; the company could thus be liable for any statements Andy might make to the media. In fact, Klein advised Andy not to speak to the media at all. But Andy countered that it wasn't every day a small beer company got a call from a large network. Besides, Andy went on, he thought he could control what he said.

In the end, Andy's argument beat Klein's, and I went on the air. The Fox interview generated even more publicity—this time in the *New York Post*—and I was happy to exploit it.

The next call, however, was from the SEC. Ralph Norman, the regulator in charge of our filing, was not happy about the media coverage, our toll-free phone message, or our behavior in general. In fact, Mr. Norman threatened to sanction us as a way to demonstrate his extreme disapproval.

I apologized profusely and managed to convince Mr. Norman that I had erred badly out of excitement and ignorance, but that I had not actually harmed anyone. I promised I would zip my lip, media-wise, until our stock sale was over. In the end, the SEC gave Spring Street a very sharp slap on the wrist and a firm warning that dire consequences would ensue if we did not stay mute until the registration process was complete.

We had filed our documents at the end of November 1994. Registration and approval typically take anywhere from six to eight weeks.

It would be mid-January or even February of 1995 before we could do anything more. The timing suited me just fine, as Liesbeth and I were off to New Zealand. Our friend Russell, my old soccer-playing pal, the one who had been present at the creation when I announced my *witbier* future, was getting married. His coming to my wedding had sparked the idea for my change of career. As it turned out, my going to his wedding would spark yet another idea, one that would change more than my career. Much more.

9.

The Internet Breakthrough

It's a flight of more than eighteen hours from Auckland International Airport in New Zealand to JFK in New York. Even with a movie, meals, and magazines, there are stretches of downtime. At 37,000 feet, your mind is definitely in the clouds. The brain rambles onto easy abstractions, especially after it has spent days guiding the body through happy, hectic festivities, absorbing exotic sights and sounds while trying to remember a million new names and faces. Somewhere over the vastness of the Pacific Ocean, the *Wired* magazine I had been reading slipped out of my hands onto my lap, my eyes wandered out the window, and I began to ponder the strange set of occurrences that had put me on this plane at this moment.

So many things had to happen for me to be here. Soccer. England. Meeting Russell. Befriending Russell. Russell's romance, a tale built entirely on accident.

Some six years previously, he and another New Zealander were hitchhiking in Thailand when the truck in which they were riding picked up two more hitchhikers, a couple of blonde Scandinavian women—one Norwegian and one Swedish, both beautiful. Shyness prevailed in the back of the truck, however, and nobody said very much. All Russell remembers of the encounter, in fact, is that they learned that the Norwegian woman was named Karin. Then, four days later, the two sets of hitchhikers ran into one another again, in another part of Thailand. This time, their former acquaintance provided the impetus for a few words of conversation before they went their separate ways.

Five years passed. The scene switched from the Thai tropics to the London underground, where Russell's New Zealand buddy and the Swedish woman very nearly bumped into each other on the platform of the Northern Line. This coincidence was enough to lead to further meetings. The two fell in love, and when they married two years later in Sweden, Russell attended the wedding. So did the Norwegian woman. Karin. And then of course, Russell and Karin fell in love. It was their wedding in New Zealand Liesbeth and I had just attended.

What are the chances, I wondered to myself as the huge 747 rushed across the sky, of any one of these coincidences happening—much less all of them? Then add in the coincidences that made me part of the picture. How utterly random, unpredictable, and serendipitous that a Maori from New Zealand and a Norwegian from the frozen North should find themselves in the same moment in the same place in Thailand, that they should meet again, that a guy from New Jersey should find himself playing soccer in London at the same time that Russell is playing soccer in London . . . and so on. If any single one of a long chain of incidences and coincidences had not happened, the chain itself would have led somewhere else, and I would not be in the exact spot and situation I was in now—flying halfway around the world, returning to a beer business for which I needed to raise money, reading a magazine inspired by the Internet.

Pow. The idea hit me just that fast and hard, startling my mind out of its dreamy, directionless roaming. The Internet. Why not? Why not use cyberspace, the fabulous new medium of universal communication, to distribute our Wit Beer prospectus to potential Wit Beer shareholders? Just put it out there on the World Wide Web, announce that we're doing a stock offering, and let anybody who is interested download the prospectus and check it out at leisure. Free.

Back in New York, the idea made even more sense, especially

when I put it to Tim Klem, my invaluable right-hand man at the Wit office. While my own involvement with computers could be described as literate, it was hardly cutting edge. Tim, by contrast, had literally grown up "plugged in." He had gotten his first Mac while he was in elementary school, and he was not just a Web surfer but a potential Web programmer, already familiar with the basics of its hypertext markup programming language—HTML.

For some months now, in fact, Tim had been monitoring Internet chat rooms where the subject of microbrewed beers was "discussed." He had quickly realized that plugging into these sites would give us access to thousands—perhaps tens of thousands—of beer enthusiasts who just might be interested in owning a little piece of Spring Street Brewing.

We thereupon spent a long weekend separately searching the Web to assess the marketing prospects for Spring Street stock in cyberspace. When we got together on Monday morning, we were more excited than ever, for we had both come to a simple but powerful conclusion: the profile of the typical Internet browser and the profile of the typical potential Wit customer were one and the same. In short, our customers were us: young, well educated, Internet-generation males with a penchant for surfing cyberspace and for drinking craft beer—often at the same time. It made perfect sense to use the Internet to get the word out to these guys that we were offering our stock for sale.

The next step was to create a Web site. We didn't need anything fancy; in fact, "fancy" would have been the wrong way to go. Instead, we created a simple collage of photographs: Wit labels, the product itself, pictures of the master brewers. We put up a text narrative telling *witbier*'s history and the story of the founding of Wit. The stock offering was described in a separate section that more or less replicated the postcards and posters we were trying to distribute.

"Public Stock Offering," this section proclaimed. "Spring Street Brewing Company, Inc., American microbrewer of classic Belgian-recipe beer, including Wit and New Amber Wit, announces the public offering of up to 2,702,700 shares of common stock at $1.85 per share. Minimum purchase 150 shares."

But instead of an 800 number to phone, this section offered a button—a hyperlink to another site where the prospectus was replicated as a word-processing document. That meant that all the Web browser had to do was click on the button to view the prospectus, download it, and print it. The printed version included a subscription agreement; anyone wanting to buy Wit stock could fill it out and send it to us—with a check.

It was an absolutely straightforward and perfectly simple statement of our offering. It was also cheap. Apart from renting the site for perhaps $200 a month, we incurred no expenses for printing, mailing, or toll-free calls, and of course we paid not one penny in commissions to investment bankers, brokers, or securities lawyers. Two hundred bucks a month is not too much to pay to reach, potentially, the entire planet—subject to securities regulations.

Speaking of securities regulations, it seemed a good idea, given our last brush with the SEC, to run the idea past them. So I called Ralph Norman, our local examiner.

"You want to do what?" Norman's first response was cautious.

"The Internet," I told him. "The World Wide Web."

"You had better slow down," said Norman. "Hold off. Let me look into this first. I'll call you back."

I only had to sweat it out for a few hours. Norman, it turns out, was an AOL subscriber and liked browsing the Internet himself. What's more, he liked my idea of using cyberspace to sell stock, and he gave me full credit for proposing it. So the phone call that came later that day had good news. As it was, Norman informed me, the SEC nearly a year earlier had issued a release that effectively gave approval to the electronic delivery of official documents—including prospectuses. Norman didn't think there would be any trouble in proceeding with the digital offering as long as the format of the documents on the Web mirrored the paper version of the papers that had been filed off-line.

A few days later, on February 6, 1995, the SEC formally qualified our offering documents. It was the go-ahead to start selling shares.

Spring Street Brewing Company issued a triumphant press release announcing that the world's first Internet public stock offering was open for business. Our claim to be "the first" was bold, to be sure, but by now we had learned one basic fact of business life: we were never going to hit a home run if we were afraid to swing the bat.

On the first day of the offering, Tim and I busied ourselves preparing a direct mailing to our existing database—including, among others, the six thousand callers who had responded to our initial 800-number phone offering. We had the leisure to get every word right; there was not a single nibble for the Internet announcement.

The following day, however, a reporter from the *Wall Street Journal* picked up our release and invited himself to the office. Nothing in what he saw could have been less *Wall Street Journal*–ish: Tim and I were outfitted, as usual, in blue jeans and Wit T-shirts, and our leading-edge computers hadn't been on the leading edge for a number of years. Still, the reporter asked an hour's worth of questions, was given a demo of the Web site, even tasted our beer. Then, looking vaguely amused by what he had seen, he disappeared.

Two days later, the paper published his article. It was fantastic. Not only did the *Journal* reporter applaud our use of the Internet; he also confirmed, based on his own research, that ours was the first-ever Internet stock offering.

Verification and praise from the nation's most influential business paper made for a good day in our Spring Street office.

The next morning brought an even better day. Messages on the machine from more than two dozen journalists made it clear that the *Journal* wasn't the only paper to respond to our press release. The news was picked up by hundreds of newspapers and magazines across the country eager to get in on this story of a microbrewery taking itself public on the Internet. Within days, the story was running in literally hundreds of newspapers and magazines nationwide.

The *New York Times* had it. So did the *Daily News* and the *Post*,

New York's other dailies. The *Washington Post's* article was down-right glowing. Then dozens of other major city newspapers followed the lead of Washington and New York.

Business Week led the magazines in sending a reporter to profile our offering. Both *Entrepreneur* and *Success* called for interviews.

Wired magazine, voice of the Internet generation, ran a quarter-page piece with one of its zany art features: a photograph of me with a six-pack of Wit Beer somehow falling off my head. Great publicity. Our stack of clippings from the print media rose higher by the day.

Perhaps more pertinent from our perspective was coverage of the story where it counted most: on the Internet itself. The arbiters of what's cool in cyberspace loved us; search engines such as Netscape and Yahoo featured our story in vivid hyperlinks. In fact, we were on Netscape's *What's New* list for ten days, and we were on its *What's Cool* list for two years.

Best of all, of course, was the response from the people we were trying to reach: the Internet browsers/potential Wit stock buyers who were the target of our offering. From the very beginning, our makeshift Web site received constant "hits"; tens of thousands of Net tourists passed through and clicked onto the prospectus link for a closer look. I could not have been more pleased with what was happening, nor more dumbstruck with wonderment. What impelled people to take risks on the basis of free-floating information in a medium most others still did not even understand, much less trust?

Whatever the psychology behind it, the Web seemed to be just the right place in which people could most readily identify with what we were trying to do with our Internet public offering. In any event, identify they did.

Every day at around noon, the mailman arrived at our office to deliver a pile of envelopes containing checks and subscription agreements.

Not surprisingly, most of our checkwriters were beer enthusiasts, some from as far away as South Africa, Iceland, even the Far East. When you see a guy in Reykjavik trying to invest $277.50 for stock in a beer he's never seen or tasted, you got a sense of the power of the Internet.

We set up a bank account for the money and created a database of our stockholders. The database was programmed in such a way that the information was fed immediately to a certificate-printing facility. All we had to do was push a button to print out a stock certificate, which we then sent to the new stockholder.

Although we raised most of the money we sought in the first few weeks of the Web site's existence—thanks no doubt to the burst of publicity that followed our press release—we kept the site and the offering open for several months. By the time we closed, we had thirty-five hundred new stockholders and fresh capital totaling $1.6 million—the seeds of a viable marketing and sales initiative and, although I did not see it at the time, the seeds also of a revolution in the way capital can be raised.

10.

Trading Places

With our coffers filled, I was again free to focus on beer. Spring Street Brewing Company now had the wherewithal to hire additional staff and undertake marketing initiatives. We still did not have money for a big-time sales initiative, but with long hours and all the creativity we could muster, we were able to increase first quarter sales by 400 percent, a pretty fair return on our expenditure of money, time, and effort. There was no reason to think that my life or the entire Wit venture would be anything other than business as usual: hard work, inventive marketing, incremental growth.

Then we began to notice something funny. Even though our stock offering was closed, Web browsers kept logging onto our site and inquiring, via E-mail, where and how they could get hold of Wit stock. Thousands of Web browsers. Maybe they had read about the offering or had heard our story from someone, or perhaps they had drunk our beer from one of the bottles labeled with the Web address, or maybe they were just tickled by the notion of buying stock over the Internet. Whatever the reasons, the traffic in would-be stockholders continued apace—for six months, seven months, eight months, ten months after our offering. We received an awful lot of messages from people saying how disappointed they were that they could not find our stock.

We were not about to do another stock offering. And of course, the offering we had done had been that interesting little hybrid—a public offering of illiquid stock, with no secondary trading on public markets like the New York Stock Exchange or the NASDAQ market. All our buyers understood that. But seeing the ongoing interest in our stock gave me another idea. Maybe we could use the Internet to create a trading mechanism whereby people who wanted to own the stock could buy it from people who already had it.

Such Internet trading, I guessed, would cost us little to engineer. I also reasoned that putting a little trading mechanism up on the Internet could be another public relations coup. And if a flurry of media interest could ignite a new burst of sales activity, so much the better. By now, I had become a true believer in the power of media publicity and in the potential of its ripple effect. Since we didn't have the resources to buy big advertising, we were forced to get it for free by stirring journalistic interest. I have to confess I thought we were getting pretty good at it, and I saw the Internet trading mechanism as the next big story for Wit Beer.

So I went to the computer section of the nearest bookstore and bought a more advanced book on programming in hypertext markup language—HTML, the language of Web site operations, Web page creation, and hyperlinks. The plan was simple: We would create a Web site, called Wit-Trade, where buyers and sellers of Spring Street shares could find each other. Wit-Trade would be a matchmaker, pairing buyers with sellers.

To make the matches, we would build a system with two sets of bulletin boards, one for Wit stockholders interested in selling, and one for buyers interested in becoming stockholders. These bulletin boards would be just what the name implies: places to post public messages, to read the messages, and, if you like, to answer a message by posting your response. Here's how we programmed Wit-Trade's bulletin boards to work:

Say you were a buyer interested in purchasing Wit stock. You'd go to the Wit-Trade site and link up to the buyers' bulletin board. There, you would type in your name, E-mail address, number of shares you wanted to buy, and the price you were willing to pay. Then you had two choices. You could sit back and wait for a seller to respond to your notice, or, if you were a bit more aggressive, you could click onto the sellers' bulletin board. There, would-be sellers of Wit stock would have done the reverse of what you did on the buyers' bulletin board. After typing in their name and E-mail address, they would have indicated the number of shares they wanted to sell and the price they were asking. If you, the buyer, saw a deal that interested you on the sellers' bulletin board, you would just click on that entry and open an E-mail dialogue with the person who had posted the sell offer. Obviously, a would-be seller of Wit stock had the same choice of actions: either post a sell offer and passively await the buyer's call, or click over to the buyers' bulletin board to look for a trade.

Having made the match, Wit-Trade would step back and leave it to buyer and seller to negotiate a deal. They might do this entirely on our system, via E-mail, or they might go off-line to the telephone or fax machine or even a personal meeting—preferably in a tavern over Wit Beer. If buyer and seller agreed to do a trade, we would step back in to provide on-line what we called a form of offer and acceptance—really a contract through which the participants would bind themselves to the transaction. The offer and acceptance form laid out the terms of the agreement and could be E-mailed back and forth. Once both buyer and seller had accepted the offer, they essentially had a legal obligation to buy or sell Wit stock at a particular price.

At this point, Wit-Trade would act as clearing agent for the transaction. Our aim was to protect buyers from sellers and sellers from buyers, to serve as a fire wall of security for both participants in the deal by becoming middlemen. The buyer would send his check to us, Wit Beer. We would then deposit it and wait for it to clear. Meanwhile, the seller would have sent us his stock certificate, duly endorsed. We would hold on to the certificate until the buyer's check had cleared through the bank. Once that happened, we would issue a new stock certificate to the buyer, send money to the seller, and toss stock certificate in the archives. Everybody would be happy. Buyer and seller would be happy with their deal, happy with each other, and happy with Wit Beer, which was providing this wonderful, investor-friendly service.

An essential part of the service was the company financial information we decided to put on-line. The reasons were obvious. That Web browser who had read something somewhere about Wit Beer stock was not going to buy the stock solely on the basis of a vaguely remembered newspaper story or word of mouth from a fellow beer drinker in a bar. He or she would need something more than that—hard facts and figures at the very least. Typically, an interested buyer of an obscure small company's stock calls or writes the company and asks for a copy of the financials. That's flattering, but with a mailing costing a dollar or two, the costs can mount. In fact, the more interest there is in a company, the more it can cost the company.

For a small company, this can pose a real dilemma. Suppose a small company runs an ad that engenders a couple of thousand requests for information. Or suppose, as happened with Wit, a favorable article appears in a newspaper, or the company is featured on CNN. The result might be hundreds of thousands—even millions—of people interested in the company. If they are interested enough to ask to see the company's quarterly report, or annual report, or any recent press releases about company activities, what is the company to do? Remember: Most if not all of the people making the requests for printed materials will probably not buy a single share of company stock. Even if they do, the company gains no revenue from the purchase as it is simply facilitating secondary trading of the stock, not issuing stock through a public offering. There's the dilemma: Saying no to such requests is bad for the company image and ultimately bad for business. After all, the company is the only source of the financial information these hundreds of thousands or millions of people are now clamoring for. On the other hand, satisfying their demands—and paying for printing, copying, distribution, and postage—will simply bankrupt the small company.

Wit-Trade solved that dilemma, at least vis-à-vis Internet-savvy investors. With a click of the mouse, anybody could sign on to Wit-Trade and, at no cost, view our financial reports. I mean all of it: the annual reports audited by our accountants at Arthur Andersen, up-to-date quarterly financial reports, even press releases about new activities and developments. Potential investors could not just access this information; they could download it, print it out, export the information to spreadsheets where they could massage the data any which way they liked. As if that weren't enough, we also built a kind of ticker tape onto the site, a stream of information that would show the volume of Wit stock trading through Wit-Trade, the price, and the high and low buy and sell offers for the last period. The bottom line of all this information was a clear picture of Wit Beer and the Spring Street Brewing Company: sales, contracts, performance, marketplace data, stock price, stock activity, stock liquidity, and more—plenty of information for making an informed, intelligent decision.

The plan was to launch Wit-Trade on March 1, 1996, a Friday. We would give the launch a lavish send-off with a party scheduled for Thursday night, Leap Year's February 29, at @Café, a street-level electronic bar in the East Village section of New York. Our press release heralded Wit-Trade as "the first-ever digital stock market," described the mechanism in detail, and invited journalists to come to the party and have the first look at a live demonstration of how it would operate.

The press response was fantastic. In addition to dozens of print journalists, three television news crews showed up to film the event. The party on February 29 was a wild success, and so was the news coverage on March 1. Television newscasts, the *Wall Street Journal*, *USA Today*, the wire services, and hundreds of business news columnists claimed that Wit-Trade was a first in electronic history. Within hours of launching the system, literally tens of thousands of people had visited the Wit-Trade Web site and looked at our materials. The bulletin boards hummed with names and offers.

It was a highly celebratory weekend for all of us at Wit Beer. But

Monday morning arrived quickly. At about 11:00 A.M., the phone rang in the Spring Street office. The caller was a staff lawyer at the SEC. Could Mr. Klein please stand by for a conference call that afternoon? The commission would like to discuss the matter of Wit-Trade.

Uh oh.

11.

A Heavy Date with the Stock Cops

The conference call got under way at four that afternoon. The first fifteen minutes of the call were taken up with introductions. I stated my name, and so did the SEC lawyers—I stopped counting at eleven. There was the chief of corporate finance and the chief legal counsel, the head of stock exchange regulation, the head of clearing firm regulation, the head of market manipulation, and the head of broker-dealer registration. Supporting the chiefs and heads were countless deputies, assistants, and deputy assistants.

For the next two hours, I tried frantically to transcribe the blizzard of questions precipitated by this veritable synod of attorneys. They needed answers to the questions, they said, in order to determine whether they were right in thinking that Wit-Trade had no business doing what it was doing. Occasionally, when I was able to get a word in edgewise, I argued that Wit-Trade was simply a convenient, low-cost way to promote a beer company and facilitate fair trading in its stock. That was a legal objective, I asserted, essentially no different from the kinds of things small public companies do every day to enhance liquidity in their shares. The use of the Internet, I suggested, was a logistical matter that only made it more likely that our efforts would work. What seemed a sensible argument in my head began to sound like a desperate protestation of innocence when I said it out loud.

What's more, the argument scored no points with the SEC legal team. As they vied with one another to suggest regulations Wit-Trade might possibly be violating, they seemed also to be labeling our actions as not just imprudent but impudent as well. The tone from many of the lawyers was one of astonishment at best, annoyance at worst, that a tiny beer company was causing all this hullabaloo in the first place.

On the imprudent front, what concerned the SEC lawyers was the possibility that Wit-Trade might in some way, shape, or form constitute a brokerage house or stock exchange. If that were the case, we would be subject to government regulation, formidable capital requirements, as well as to a variety of legal conditions, provisions, and stipulations. The SEC lawyers also voiced a concern that the highly public, easily accessible Web pages on which bids and orders were posted could be vulnerable to manipulation by unscrupulous Web browsers.

But while the lawyers were crisply precise when it came to noting the problems Wit-Trade had surfaced, they were uncharacteristically taciturn when it came to volunteering any solutions. Profligate with their questions, they were stingy with their answers. At six in the evening, I finally asked, "What do you want me to do?" The convocation of attorneys gave a unanimous three-word answer.

"We don't know," the SEC lawyers admitted. By a kind of unhappy default, it was thus agreed that Wit-Trade, however slight its chances for ultimately surviving regulatory scrutiny, could continue to operate for a day or two while the SEC lawyers continued to study the matter.

Three days later, there was another conference call—with only six lawyers this time, but with the same results. The SEC was still "studying the matter." Its lawyers were not prepared to tell me what was wrong with Wit-Trade. In fact, they were not prepared to tell me whether *anything* was wrong with Wit-Trade. In the kind of deliberate circumlocution I had myself mastered as a lawyer at Cravath, Swaine & Moore, they hedged, prevaricated, came down squarely in the middle, and took up a seated position right smack dab on the fence. They simply did not know what to tell me. This business of the Internet was new to them. The innovation of Wit-Trade was new to them. There were no precedents. What's more, the whole situation carried the unmistakable odor of "high tech," something foreign, untested, unexplored, and therefore, to some extent, unintelligible.

But while they studied the matter, while they tentatively probed at the edge of what might potentially be a whole new field for the agency's scrutiny, they did have some advice for me. In effect, their message was that I should shut down Wit-Trade while they applied themselves to finding and defining the crime I would be committing if I did not shut down Wit-Trade.

I confess I got pretty hot under the collar at this point. It was fine for the SEC lawyers to debate abstractions; they had all the time in the world. But if I shut down, my entire experiment in creating liquidity for Spring Street's shareholders would be finished. I could deal with specific allegations of violations of statutory regulations—if we had broken a law, we had broken a law. But "Just stop what you're doing" did not strike me as fair or sensible regulatory intervention.

My argument to this effect fell on deaf ears. In fact, the lawyers told me I should consider myself lucky. "You don't realize," they said, "that people don't usually get legal advice from the SEC." What was their legal advice? It was that I should hire lawyers who specialized in dealing with the SEC. I knew all about such lawyers. For example, I knew that it would cost tens of thousands of dollars to retain them to argue my case. This was not a viable option.

"Are you ordering me to shut down Wit-Trade?" I asked the lawyers. "Not really," came the reply. So I didn't. "We'll get back to you," the lawyers said, "by week's end." There was a strong implication that I should be prepared for unfavorable news.

To be fair, I believe that the SEC staff was actually fairly sympathetic to our cause. They certainly understood that Spring Street was a small company with limited resources. They also agreed that our only objective had been to use new technology creatively to construct an environment in which our shareholders might find liquidity and thus enhance the value of their stock holdings. Throughout, everyone from the SEC staff dealt with us honestly and straightforwardly; our exchanges had never been unfriendly, only frustrating.

At the same time, however, I sensed a certain discomfort on their part. After all, Wit-Trade could prove to be one of those breakthrough innovations that challenged the agency to question its competence to enforce the securities laws in an age of digital technology.

One thing was absolutely certain: I did not want to fight the SEC. It had power, time, and virtually limitless resources. I couldn't win.

Gloom descended on the Spring Street office. To think that our lovely little microbrewery might come unglued because of an SEC ruling was a dismal, depressing thought. At best, we would have to come up with some other way to create liquidity for our shareholders. But the idea for Wit-Trade had come at wit's end; I could not imagine that I would be lucky enough to have another brainstorm if this one got shot out from under me.

The air of melancholy hung heavy all day following that second, heated conference call. We sweated it out till late in the afternoon, when the phone rang with another call from the SEC. This time, however, the caller was Steven Wallman, one of the five SEC commissioners, each of them appointed directly by the president of the United States.

Before his appointment, Wallman, like most SEC commissioners, had been a partner in the securities practice of a major law firm—in his case, the prestigious Washington firm, Covington & Burling. Unlike any other SEC commissioner, however, Wallman's previous life included a stint as a techie, a student of computer science as an undergraduate at M.I.T. So when Wallman noticed the staff activity over Wit-Trade, he decided to take a personal interest in the matter. His personal interest would change my life.

"I think what you have done is very interesting," the commissioner said once the introductions were concluded. "And I see no reason why the SEC and Spring Street Brewing cannot find common ground."

Music to my ears.

"While it's true there are people here who think your operation should be stopped cold," the commissioner continued, "there are others who think Wit-Trade is an important experiment, the type of entrepreneurial activity that should be encouraged. The agency is not hostile to the technology, to the Internet, or to small companies finding creative ways to raise capital or facilitate trading in their shares. But there are securities laws on the books that have been put there for good reason, and it is our job to make sure they are followed and enforced."

Then came a startling proposition: "If you voluntarily suspend the trading mechanism," Wallman said, "I would like to work with you toward a resolution that would allow you to use the Internet to create a trading environment for your shareholders. Stop the trading system for now and I promise to get back to you with real guidance on how to operate it without violating the federal securities laws."

It was the proverbial "offer I couldn't refuse." I thanked Commissioner Wallman as warmly as I knew how and immediately shuttered Wit-Trade. I also fired up the mighty Wit publicity machine—i.e., me and my PC—and issued a press release announcing that the SEC had asked us to back off during its review of Wit-Trade. Spirits around the office rose at once; action had been taken that could once again put us in the public eye.

We got the release out the next day. The press response that followed was stunning. With the SEC spotlight shining on our innocent faces, this new episode in the Wit story hit the *Wall Street Journal*, *USA Today*, the *New York Times*, the Associated Press, CNN, CNBC, NBC, and the financial presses in Great Britain, Japan, and Spain. When it was all over, our story had been told in some fifty countries.

The SEC intervention had moved our story off the feature page into the news section. We had become breaking news, and every action and response now became another event in the story, qualifying us for almost daily news coverage. Over the next couple of weeks, we milked this reality for all it was worth. Reporters of every stripe began descending on our tiny corporate office. Flashbulbs popped, and in every photograph I was wearing a Wit cap, holding a frosty bottle of Wit Beer, or sitting in front of the computer screen so the camera could capture the large red-and-orange logo the Mezzina/Brown team had devised for Wit-Trade.

As one might expect, more news coverage meant more beer sales. It also meant thousands more hits on our Web page. So far, the wait for the SEC ruling, enriched by the image of Wit Beer David against SEC Goliath, was turning out to be very good for business.

Two weeks after Commissioner Wallman's call, the SEC's resolution of the matter came to us over the office fax. We huddled around the machine, trying to read Wit-Trade's fate upside down and backwards. When we finally ripped the page from the out tray, it turned out that any way you looked at it, we had scored a pretty impressive triumph. The SEC's letter opened with such lavish praise for "our nation's financial innovators"—to wit, us—that I positively blushed as I read it. It went on to award us permission to resume trading our stock on Wit-Trade's electronic bulletin boards—subject to certain modifications.

First, Spring Street Brewing Company could neither hold nor control investors' money; instead, we had to arrange for the funds to be held in escrow by a bank or other competent (i.e., regulated) entity.

Second, we were to disclose to investors in a more effective way that the securities being traded were potentially illiquid and speculative.

Third, we were to give investors access to a record of the volumes and prices of recent purchases and sales executed by the system.

Fourth and finally, we were to subject to SEC regulatory scrutiny the financial statements and other information about Spring Street that were being provided on the Web site.

Even before the ink was dry on the fax, I was thanking our lucky stars—and Commissioner Steven Wallman. I sat down to write a press release: "SEC Conditionally Approves Digital Stock Trading."

The press release registered a ten-plus on the Richter scale of media uproar. Headlines informed the planet—and I do mean planet—that the SEC had not just vindicated a little beer company but had officially approved Web-based stock trading. "Extraordinary," said the *Wall Street Journal*, not exactly known for its effusive language, while *USA Today* dubbed Wit "a Wall Street pioneer."

The theme of innovative enterprise resounded around the world. In only three weeks, more than fifteen hundred stories covered the subject. Not a day went by that a television crew didn't show up at the Spring Street office. We stumbled over cables and shaded our eyes from the glaring lights. And then we watched ourselves on *CNN Headline News*, the *CBS Evening News* with Dan Rather, CNBC— three times—and *Fox TV National News*. We never did get to see ourselves on the national networks of Spain, Germany, the Netherlands, or Japan. But we were there.

When we weren't looking at ourselves on television, we were reading about ourselves in full-page spreads in every major financial magazine you could think of: *Business Week, Fortune, Forbes, Inc., Entrepreneur, Kiplinger*, and *Smart Money*, to name just some of them.

And when we weren't looking at or reading our story, we were talking more about it, responding to literally tens of thousands of phone calls and E-mail messages and faxes. In the first two weeks alone, some six hundred companies called to ask us to help them raise money over the Internet, or for assistance in setting up their own electronic trading systems.

And almost daily, dozens of business plans and financing proposals started showing up in our mailbox. Individual retail investors by the thousands posted E-mail messages expressing interest in what we had done. Thousands more phoned the office to inquire when they could buy or trade our stock without having to apply to brokers or pay commissions.

Then came a number of intriguing phone calls from such technology companies as America On-Line and IBM, from such investment banks as Bear Stearns and Morgan Stanley, and from a number of discount brokerage firms that were themselves exploring Internet trading: E-Trade, Lombard Securities, E-Broker.

A lot of these people said they'd like to come by the office, meet with me, and see our technology setup. So I spent a couple of weeks greeting these visitors from as far away as Omaha, Nebraska, and, of course, Silicon Valley, California. I answered and asked questions, I looked at the technology they wanted to show us, and I showed them the technology we had. A lot of them were awfully surprised at the simplicity of our setup. Most of these companies had invested millions of dollars in sophisticated electronic systems, and here was our little Wit-Trade mechanism, created with plain old HTML programming language at a cost of a few hundred bucks. They paid close and serious attention.

It all made for an extremely exciting couple of weeks. And when the visitors had gone home and the television camera crews had packed up their cables and left, we were finally free to celebrate the sweetness of our victory and concentrate on what was really at issue—trading our stock on the Internet.

Except that I was beginning to think that was not really the issue at all. There was another issue here—something bigger than Wit-Trade. Wit-Trade, in fact, now appeared to me to be just the tip of the iceberg. Underneath it, a huge opportunity lurked, a unique way of raising capital from individual investors through the Internet, and perhaps too a whole new way for public stocks to trade. With its simple, static HTML bulletin boards, Wit-Trade was all of a sudden looking small, limited. A far more sophisticated, far more consequential idea had captured my imagination.

12.

From Brewer to Banker

The idea that was brewing in my mind had nothing to do with beer. It was about something else altogether, about a whole new way for ordinary people to become stock investors. Almost by accident, our initial public offering for Spring Street Brewing and our hasty construction of the Wit-Trade enterprise had shown that you could use Internet technology both to offer stock and to trade it. Why not put that model to work for other companies?

Spring Street's initial public offering had shown that the Internet was the perfect medium through which a small, early-stage enterprise could find and reach potential investors—people knowledgeable about the enterprise's product and willing to risk a small investment for a potentially high return. The Spring Street experiment had demonstrated that you could do this cheaply, without using brokers, and without having to print and mail prospectuses.

Why couldn't the same model be applied to other companies? Other early-stage companies could also avoid venture capitalists and tap directly and digitally into a pool of affinity investors via the Internet. And it wasn't just entrepreneurial, developing companies that could benefit from the model; why should even large, mature companies print and mail offering documents if they could reach enough investors on-line?

Similarly, Wit-Trade had shown you could use the Internet to provide moderate liquidity. Would-be buyers and would-be sellers of Spring Street stock had met over the Internet to buy, sell, and swap stock without needing to go through brokers, or deal with dealers, or have a seat on the stock exchange. They saved the fees and commissions, and, by executing trades directly with other investors, they avoided the spreads charged by market makers and specialists who are the middlemen of every traditional stock market trade.

Why couldn't that model work as a trading mechanism for other companies, too? In a digital trading market, investors could deal directly with one another to buy or sell the shares of all sorts of companies—at better prices than the traditional markets could ensure. And if they traded stocks that way, why couldn't they also trade all sorts of securities that way—digitally, and directly with other investors?

There was a circular inevitability about this model. Build a community of investors on the World Wide Web, and they will come. And when they come—real investors, sophisticated investors in the thousands and tens of thousands—then the major corporations issuing stock would come there, too, knowing they could find on the Web a base of stable investors from whom they might raise funds at fair but competitive rates. The more corporations come looking for investors, the more investors will be lured there as well. And so on.

It's simple. Connect people looking to raise capital with investors looking for places to put their money. Directly. Connect people looking to buy stocks with others looking to sell stocks. Directly.

For if there was a single theme that had emerged over the past few weeks, standing out like a bright red thread in a tapestry of pale gray, it was this: An increasingly large community of investors wanted an alternative to traditional capital markets with all their middlemen and intermediaries and barrier builders. They wanted the kind of direct access to one another and to information that they were accustomed to getting and had come to expect from the Internet. They wanted to be wired to investment possibilities and investors—on-line, in real time.

That being the case, why not apply what had worked for Spring Street to a wider canvas?

That was the idea churning in my mind in the latter part of March 1996. It was Friday afternoon. Late. I was being interviewed by a print journalist doing a story on me using the angle that I was an innovative entrepreneur and accidental technologist. My interviewer asked if any other companies had called seeking help on using the Internet to raise capital or arrange for electronic trading of their shares.

I showed her some evidence—E-mail, snail mail, fax and phone messages—of the flood of queries and comments that had been unleashed as a result of the SEC advisory letter, some six hundred requests from business enterprises asking for information, ideas, assistance. Our correspondents ranged from a Fortune 1000 company to a small-cap venture marooned on NASDAQ, to a buffalo rancher looking to sell 20 percent of his spread.

"Do you intend to help them?" I remember the journalist asking.

"I'm already talking to one or two of the quality companies," I began. Then I added, "I think we're going to start a business around this."

I had not known I was going to say that. I had not known I was thinking it. But once I had said it, I knew it was true. And when I saw it in print in a major business publication on Monday morning, I was sure of it.

The printed remark loosed another deluge of communications. That Friday, one of the phone calls in the deluge had the effect of galvanizing me into action. The gentleman on the line was not just another prospective investor looking to put his money into something he might find on the Internet. This gentleman knew exactly what he wanted to invest in: us. He was all set to invest in this new business he had read about, the one that would use the Internet to give investors a better way to invest, the one that did not exist. Yet.

Several other prospective investors called over the next few days, also inquiring whether I intended to open an Internet investment bank and, if so, whether I sought equity backers. One of the backers was a venture capital firm in Washington, D.C., that actually had flowers delivered to the office! It was certainly the most ornamental response I had ever had from venture capital investors.

Hearing from people who want to invest their money in you will concentrate the mind wonderfully. I locked myself away one weekend and forced myself to think through the half-formed notions that were churning in my brain. Then I crystallized my thinking in the form of a business plan, one calling for the creation of a whole new company.

What I proposed was nothing less than an investment bank and brokerage firm that would arrange stock offerings and facilitate stock trading over the Internet and the World Wide Web.

This company would let early-stage companies and noninstitutional investors meet directly, on their own level playing field in cyberspace, thus creating a more efficient model for capital formation than any that existed to date.

The company would develop a digital stock market in which stock sellers and buyers would interact directly, thus avoiding the spreads imposed by traditional market makers and specialists.

For retail investors who resented being excluded from the old-boy network that distributes the best stocks to wealthy individuals and institutions, my putative company offered an unprecedented opportunity for an equal shot at IPOs. That alone could attract a large pool of prospective investors to the new on-line investment community.

For small-cap companies that sought alternatives to traditional venture capital yet could not afford the high cost of printed prospectuses and lavish road shows, that pool of prospective retail investors represented a ready-made, highly attractive source of growth capital.

And it was all possible through the new medium of the Internet.

I needed a name for this proposed company, but what do you call an investment bank and trading market that grew out of a beer company? Marketing experts tell you that if you have a good brand identity, stick with it. With that in mind, Wit Capital Corporation seemed just the right moniker.

But creating a company isn't just a matter of writing a business plan. There are rules and regulations that must be followed. For one thing, a company that is going to have more than one shareholder must have more than one director. I decided to look for people whose knowledge and experience could provide both validation and substance to the idea behind the company.

My first thought was to see if I could find someone with credentials in investment banking. I happened to mention this one day to a friend of mine, and he told me about a friend of his—a very experienced, very accomplished investment banker who just might want to be a director of Wit Capital Corporation. David Blumberg had spent fourteen years at Merrill Lynch & Company, Inc., where his last position was as managing director. So he certainly knew something about investment banking. Fourteen years had been enough, however. David propelled himself out of big-name investment banking into his own little investment banking boutique. Someone with big corporate experience and a healthy restiveness about big corporate life: it sounded familiar; it made David Blumberg sound perfect.

We met. I talked about what I wanted to do. I showed David my business plan. I asked him to serve on the board of directors of Wit Capital. He agreed at once. The next day, however, he called back with an even more striking proposition: Would I be interested in naming him head of investment banking at Wit Capital and having him bring his entire practice into the new firm? I would. In a matter of minutes, David and I negotiated an equity participation and David joined the nascent firm and its board of directors.

I also went to my old Wit Beer partners, John Mezzina and Bill Brown. In the few years of our association, Mezzina/Brown had moved aggressively into the electronic design business. They had spun off a highly successful subsidiary, Mezzina/Brown Interactive, where sixty-five extremely creative people produced Web site designs and interactive graphic work. Among their clients were Sony, Intel, *Newsweek*, and Walt Disney World—a pretty high-powered list.

When I told John and Bill my idea for Wit Capital, they were as eager and excited as when I had first introduced them to *witbier*. Maybe more eager and excited. It was agreed that Bill Brown would join the board of directors and that the Mezzina/Brown ad agency and Mezzina/Brown Interactive would provide marketing, advertising, and Web design services in return for equity.

Wit Capital now had two directors. It had one of the best Web design firms in the business. It had a senior investment banker who had been a managing director at Merrill Lynch. Not a bad beginning.

A week later, I circulated the first private placement memorandum for Wit Capital Corporation. As required by law, the distribution was limited to investors with assets of at least $1 million or an income of not less than $200,000 per year and the reasonable expectation that that income would continue. At the top of my distribution list for the memo were those investors who had offered to invest in the company before it ever existed. I figured they would be particularly interested. And they were.

Over the next week, several of them, as well as other prospective investors, came to the Spring Street offices to have a look around and talk with David and me. We had cleared out the back storage room, and it was now the headquarters of Wit Capital. There, among cartons of beer, stacks of promotional T-shirts, and boxes of pint glasses, ensconced on the old folding chairs around a metal table from Staples, David and I shared our vision of the future and our financial projections with these prospective investors.

Within ten days, an initial group had committed to buy 10 percent of Wit Capital for $1 million.

13.

A Crash Course about How Stocks Trade

With money in the bank and the summer just getting under way, David and I threw ourselves into the job of business building.

As had been the case with beer, the first item on the agenda was education. In this case, however, the subject matter was not hops and barley but stock trading—a world about which I knew virtually nothing, despite having spent seven years as a securities lawyer.

We started with the basics, with the investors who want to buy or sell securities. To do that, they place orders through brokers. The brokers are agents who earn commissions in exchange for routing their customers' orders to a marketplace.

There are two types of marketplaces for stock trading in the United States, and the way an order is executed depends on the type of marketplace—whether a stock exchange or dealer market.

In a stock exchange, like the New York Stock Exchange, the broker routes all the orders relating to a particular stock to a specialist. Specialists are people assigned to particular securities; their job is to facilitate the trading in their stocks. They then attempt to match the orders routed to them by brokers—a buy order with a sell order. If no such match is readily available, the specialist will trade against the order for his or her own account, acting as principal in the transaction.

In a dealer market, like NASDAQ, the order can be routed to any one of the securities firms that regularly trades in the security. These firms, which also buy or sell shares as principals, not agents, are called market makers.

Both specialists and market makers charge for shares traded through them. This charge, called the "spread," is the difference between the bid price for which specialists and market makers offer to buy the stock and the ask price they set to sell the stock. They're entitled to this spread, or so they say as justification, as reward for their role in guaranteeing a stable ongoing market in the security. They do this by trading the security for their own account against any broker's orders, whether the price of the shares is moving up or down, and whatever the demand. It means that the investor, you and I, can be certain that our buy or sell orders in that stock will always be executed at once.

If the stock is very liquid—if it is trading back and forth very fast and furiously—the spread will be small, perhaps even as small as an eighth or even a sixteenth of a point on each share; if trading is sluggish, as it is for the vast majority of NASDAQ issues, the spread will be large—often as wide as 50 cents on every share and sometimes as wide as $2.

That is the basic brokerage business. It has been a good business for centuries, so it is no wonder that brokers, dealers, specialists, and market makers have been at best wary and at worst resistant to any radical changes to the business. Like the kinds of changes technological innovation can bring.

Not all technological innovation, to be sure. The industry—and the exchanges controlled by the industry—were quick to embrace technological innovation that sped the flow of transactions, of information about markets, of quotes and execution reports from the marketplaces, as well as technology that sped the transmission of brokers' orders to the marketplace.

But they discouraged and occasionally attempted to sabotage every technological innovation that threatened to alter the way in which stocks were traded. It's not surprising. Such changes, they feared—perhaps rightly—would threaten the supremacy of the brokerage firms that had been founded on and flourished within the existing system.

But like the genie that could not be put back in the bottle, technology over the past twenty years managed to create a variety of computer-based trading systems that essentially cut out the specialists and market makers. It did this by connecting buyers and sellers of stocks directly; it thus made possible transactions "within" or "between" the spread. In fact, as we learned, for institutional traders, electronic trading systems with names like Instinet, POSIT, and AZX already accounted for nearly 20 percent of the daily volume on the major stock markets.

Instinet, founded in the 1970s and today owned by Reuters PLC, the huge British multinational news and information processing conglomerate, is the biggest of the electronic trading systems for institutional traders. Using networked computers and a proprietary software, Instinet offers institutional investors an electronic order book. Trading parties simply enter their orders to buy or sell securities directly into the order book. It means that when the big institutions want to buy or sell stock, they don't call a broker who then calls a specialist or market maker. They just boot up their special computers and check the order book on the screen. If there's a sell order they'd like to take, they click on it and take it. If there's a buy order they find attractive, they click and "hit" it, as the jargon goes.

No broker, no dealer, no market-making middleman, no spread. The trade is executed directly between buyer and seller, each of whom pays Instinet a tiny fee per share traded. Today, Instinet alone does more than 15 percent of the daily volume of NASDAQ and the New York Stock Exchange.

POSIT is the second-largest electronic trading system, and it operates differently. As opposed to Instinet's hit-and-take system, POSIT uses what is called an auction or crossing mechanism. In an auction, the system collects batches of large individual orders for a specific stock, each batch with its own price range. Every so often, the system collates the batches and trades shares at a price set by an outside source—for example, the stock's current NYSE price. In practice, each individual trader gets the mean price for the stock as it is being traded at that instant on the New York Stock Exchange. POSIT does the collating four times a day, when it crosses buy and sell orders from institutions at the midpoint between the bid and ask price of the national market.

All this—and more—David and I learned that summer of study. It was stunning to consider how, when it comes to trading stocks, the huge institutions are very different from you and me. They do not use traditional brokers. They do not pay the same types of commissions. They do not route their orders to traditional marketplaces where the specialists or market makers impose a spread on every share transacted. They just match directly with other institutional investors within the spread. And the businesses that help them do it have grown huge and rich in the process.

As the hot summer wore on, my idea began to come into focus. Why couldn't we develop something comparable for individual retail investors? Create an electronic trading system that would match buyers and sellers directly, thus cutting out the middleman—disintermediating the intermediary, as the jargon had it—and saving the spread? The big electronic systems that served the institutional investors were built on proprietary networks and geared only to large block trading. Such a system would be prohibitively expensive to build and inappropriate in any case. No, my idea was to deliver the comparable model to individual investors through the Internet, an open-architecture, low-cost public medium that was perfect for the small-scale transactions that retail investors dealt in.

David and I hung up a blackboard and did some calculations. How would such a system work, and how would individual investors benefit?

Take, for example, a simple trade between Joe Smith and Jane Doe for 1,000 shares of ABC Inc. ABC trades regularly but modestly on NASDAQ, where the market makers have quoted a bid price of

$10 and an ask price of $11. That means that an investor could buy shares from the market at $11, or sell them for $10 per share. (The $1 difference is, of course, the spread earned by the market maker for providing the market.)

Joe initiates an order to sell by calling his broker—say a traditional discount broker charging him $150 to handle the trade. He handles it as an agent, sending the order to a market-maker firm, XYZ Securities. At the same time, Jane's broker has charged her a commission—let's say she uses Merrill Lynch and will pay $400 for the service—to send her buy order to the same market maker. XYZ Securities then handles the execution of both orders. It sells Jane 1,000 shares of ABC Inc. for $10 per share, or $10,000, and at the same moment (more or less), it buys the same 1,000 shares from Joe for $9 per share, or $9,000.

So Jane buys a stock for $10 a share that at that exact moment she could resell for no more than $9 a share, the brokers earn a total of $550 in commissions, and the market maker pockets a total of $1,000 as compensation for providing the marketplace.

Now compare that to the transaction Joe and Jane might have had they been mega-institutions trading through Instinet. Joe could have placed his order in an electronic order book, where he might, for example, offer to sell 1,000 shares at the midpoint between the bid and ask spread, which is $10.50. Jane, having looked in the order book to find a seller, would have seen Joe's offer, liked it, and "hit" it. End of transaction. The trade would have occurred directly between Joe and Jane at the price of $10.50 per share.

Of course, Instinet would have taken its 2 cents per share on the transaction. Assuming that was shared equally between the parties, Joe and Jane would each have incurred transaction costs of $10. That's a big savings over the costs of doing the transaction in the traditional marketplace. There, Joe and Jane lost 50 cents on every share right off the top—$500 in all—to feed the market maker's spread.

The numbers helped clarify my developing idea. This was something much bigger than Wit-Trade, much more than simply providing a modest bulletin board on which shares of obscure beer companies could trade. This was creating a whole new kind of electronic trading environment, using the Internet as the public backbone for the environment, to serve individual investors. In so doing, we would be leveling the playing field for *all* investors—individuals and institutions, zillionaires and common folk.

Chances are, not everybody was going to like the idea.

But David and I were in love with it. The task now was to find the tool that would make it all work—the right technology for the electronic trading system that we envisaged.

14.

Finding Gold in Tribeca

This is the moment in the script when one of those bizarre coincidences occurred, the kind of chance good fortune about which the Hollywood producer would say: "I'm not sure we believe this. It's a glitch in the arc of the story. Build the moment some other way." But this is exactly the way it happened.

Somewhere toward the end of that summer of 1996, a gentleman named Ed Story walked into our office. Ed had graduated from Harvard Business School and built his career in the financial services industry. Eventually, he went to work as a marketing executive at the Chicago Stock Exchange—where he had been involved in the creation of an electronic trading system called Chicago Match that had been designed to match institutional buyers with institutional sellers and thus compete head-on with Instinet.

Chicago Match had operated for less than a year and then had simply shut down. Ed Story was out of a job. He was quite literally just wandering down Spring Street that summer's day when suddenly, by coincidence or fate or chance, he remembered reading an article about Wit-Trade, with offices, he now recalled, on Spring Street, which was why Ed Story suddenly showed up out of the blue.

He was pretty straightforward. "Electronic trading is something of an arcane niche community," he said. "You probably don't know very

much about it. I do. I know a lot about it. If you want to create an Internet trading system that really works, I could help you. There is not
a lot of software out there," he continued, "but I have some ideas
about what might work for you."

"I'm listening," I said.

Ed explained that he was building a practice as a consultant to brokerage and trading firms. Although he realized we could not guaran-
tee him any long-term employment, he offered, for a short-term
contract, to take us to meet a number of software developers who
had programming code that might be useful to us. We hired him on
the spot. And with Ed as guide and navigator, we hit the road.

The first meeting that Ed arranged was with Jerry Pustilnik, who
had founded Instinet in his small office more than twenty years before. Jerry was now working out of a new electronic trading firm
based in New Jersey, but he maintained an interest in every development in institutional matching. His experience and expertise were invaluable to us.

Next stop was Bill Lupien, who had been recruited to Instinet by
its financial backers when the company was faltering in its early
years. More than any other person, Lupien had been responsible for
fueling Instinet's prodigious growth. He ran the company for two
decades until selling out to Reuters in 1988. More recently, Bill had
started a new company, OptiMark Technologies, Inc., in Durango,
Colorado. The OptiMark system, which Bill invented, is yet another
type of institutional trading system. This one, however, is based on a
super computer and has the single objective of providing large block
traders a way to program "liquidity curves." Basically, OptiMark lets
traders profile their trading strategies without disclosing them; it
then optimizes all the orders presented so that everyone who trades
in OptiMark gets optimal execution based on their own strategy profile and all the other strategy profiles in the system. It's a technically
advanced, highly sophisticated system, one that can have major impact on the marketplace.

Ed also arranged a meeting at Instinet itself, where senior management were in equal measure intrigued by and skeptical of the idea of the Internet replacing the proprietary network on which their billion-dollar-a-year business was based.

Then it was on to an entrepreneur named Steve Wunch, who had built the Arizona Stock Exchange, another institutional trading system, around single-price auction algorithms. Basically, this system batches orders to buy and sell stocks. Then, twice a day, the system crosses the orders at the single price that results in the greatest number of shares traded.

In Cleveland, Ohio, Ed put us onto a trading technology being developed by a group of former Bear Stearns techies. Another trading system, in Philadelphia, had been conceived by a group of traders with backgrounds in commodities. Out in Silicon Valley, we met with a group that had built a system for trading energy units and had some vague idea about converting it into an equity market.

And then we came home to New York and went more or less around the corner to a little company called Global Trade to meet a man named Chris Keith.

Ed had filled me in on Chris's background. He had spent nineteen years as a senior employee of the New York Stock Exchange, the last eight of them as chief of technology. He had been a founding director of the Securities Industry Automation Corporation (SIAC), which had been started for the express purpose of developing automated systems for the New York and American Stock Exchanges and the National Clearance and Settlement System. In fact, Chris had designed for SIAC most of the automated systems used by major stock exchanges to route orders, to report market data, to clear and settle securities transactions. He was responsible for the design and development of the legendary Consolidated Tape, which electronically collects and reports trades in stocks listed on the NYSE no matter in which market the trade takes place, and for the Composite Quotation system, which displays the prices and number of shares bid and asked. It sounded to me like Chris Keith, at age sixty-six, was the veritable father of electronic trading.

But that wasn't all. Before he got to the NYSE, Chris had been chief technologist at a company called Data Network Services, which was owned and operated by Automated Data Processing (ADP), which was and is the largest automated service provider to the brokerage industry. Pretty much half the brokerage firms in the country, perhaps in the world, operate off ADP technology—much of it designed by Chris Keith.

Along the way from ADP to the New York Stock Exchange, Chris's vision of electronic trading evolved. Early on, he had seen the computer as an information tool—a way to store, analyze, and massage information. Most of the applications Chris had worked on for ADP and the Stock Exchange used the computer as a database that was essentially a huge, central order book. Through the computer, you could open the order book, see what was there, and then either place an order or take an order that was pending. That was how Instinet functioned. It was also the standard operating procedure of most of the electronic trading systems Ed Story and I had looked at.

What Chris had seen, some five years previously while still at the NYSE, was that the computer was more than just an information tool. It was also a powerful communication tool. Computers networked together could talk to each other in real time, and each of those computers could hold and handle its own information. So instead of people putting their information into one computer database, any individual computer could handle the information. An investor's computer could calculate, analyze, model, and become a strategic tool, and it could talk to another computer to discuss or execute a trade. In a way, in Chris's vision, the computer stopped being just the medium of securities trading and became the message as well; the tool became the activity itself.

But when Chris pitched this vision of electronic trading to the powers that be at the NYSE, it fell on deaf ears. This was perhaps understandable. The New York Stock Exchange, as the world's most successful market, would hardly look with favor on something that was bound to diminish its significance. Yet that is precisely what

Chris's vision of the future of electronic trading threatened. The NYSE leadership can scarcely be blamed for not embracing their own potential demise.

But the wall of resistance was certainly frustrating to Chris Keith. He left the New York Stock Exchange altogether. Like many another disappointed genius, he went home, vowed to give up his dream, and instead tried to write a novel. But his very real vision of the computer as a communication device kept intruding into the fiction he was attempting to create. Chris Keith was more than ever convinced that, with the right backing and the right partners, he could build a stock market that would be vastly superior to any trading marketplace that now existed.

So after two years as a would-be novelist, Chris went to the Chicago Stock Exchange and convinced its management to fund a new kind of electronic trading mechanism. This one would combine the advantages of such electronic order book trading systems as Instinet, the features of such crossing systems as POSIT, and several new innovations based on Chris's conception of the computer not simply as database processor but as communication device.

Chris pitched the new mechanism as a quantum-leap enhancement over the first-generation electronic trading systems, a far more powerful system loaded with distinctive technological advantages that could translate into a competitive edge.

What distinguished Chris's mechanism from Instinet and other similar systems was its hybrid nature. It combined the two mechanisms already in use in the institutional electronic trading systems—the "hit-or-take" mechanism and the auction mechanism—incorporating the best features of both to become something more useful and more marketable than its institutional competitors.

Then add in the new features Chris had developed, and, as the board of the Chicago Exchange agreed, you had something really special. Among the new features of Chris's system were elaborate algorithms for conditional orders and "intelligent agents" that would ride through the process with an order and alter the character and terms of the order based on preset reactions to market pricing and other circumstances. Talk about competitive advantage.

To develop this system for the Chicago Stock Exchange Chris put together the company he called Global Trade; obviously, he was thinking big. He hired a number of his old colleagues from NYSE— among them, a fellow named Walter Buist, a name to remember.

Global Trade built Chris's system for the Chicago Stock Exchange, which they called Chicago Match, over the course of some eighteen months at a cost of more than $3 million. When the system was ready, Chris and his staff tested it, found it sound and effective, and turned it over to the Chicago Stock Exchange.

But a funny thing had happened at the top of the Chicago Exchange just as the project was being completed. The entire management team that had backed Chicago Match was kicked out. Replacing them was a new team of managers who weren't sure the exchange could or should compete with the electronic trading systems and certainly did not want to spend money trying.

So although millions had already been spent on the development of Chris's system, the new managers decided to spend just thousands to launch it.

Not surprisingly, few institutional customers materialized. While the system was enthusiastically received by technology press and the experts that studied it, the critical mass necessary to create liquidity never came. After ten feeble months of halfhearted effort, the Chicago Stock Exchange pulled the plug on Chris's trading system.

But Chris Keith did not go down the drain with it. His contract with the exchange had provided that the software rights would revert to Global Trade if the system were not used as planned. It had been a smart move by Chris's lawyers, and it yielded just about the only thing Chris walked away with from the experience. He had been paid a development salary, of course, but his deal was that he would earn royalties once the system was up and working; since it never really was up and working, Chris had made very little. But he did have the software, and he still had his firm belief that it could and would revolutionize stock trading.

When I first met Chris Keith, some four months after the software rights had reverted to him, he had been out trying to pedal the software to major brokerage firms on Wall Street. He was well received in the technology departments of such blue-chip firms as Goldman Sachs, Merrill Lynch, and Bear Stearns. All the techies, it was fair to say, waxed exceptionally enthusiastic about Chris's system. But the lengthy decision-making processes, the politics, the conflicting interests of various departments and divisions, the labyrinthine progression of a proposal up through the hierarchy were all so sluggish, so frustrating, that Chris was in danger of running out of patience. With ten developers on his payroll, he was also in real danger of running out of money. If something didn't happen soon, he would have to disband Global Trade and, very likely, give up his vision of a different kind of digital marketplace.

Enter Ed Story and Andy Klein. We didn't have far to go, either. Global Trade had offices in the Tribeca district, a stone's throw from our headquarters in Greenwich Village.

When I met Chris and saw a demonstration of the Chicago Match software, what I was looking at was a system built for big players and big money, aimed at connecting big institutions, big brokerage firms, big pension firms, big insurance companies, and big banks so that they could trade with one another, either in an auction or hit-or-take mechanism, through dial-up modems along proprietary communications networks.

"I have a question," I said to Chris when the demo was done. "Why couldn't this electronic trading system connect millions of individual retail investors over the Internet, so that they could do the kinds of things electronic trading systems already do for big institutional investors?"

"That's easy," said Chris. "It could."

Bingo.

What's more, Chris went on, it was his bet—and his firm conviction—that the Internet and his Global Trade system could create a digital stock market that could offer retail investors even greater benefits than institutional investors were today getting from the big electronic trading systems.

Wow.

The key, of course, was the use of the computer as a full-blown communications tool, one that could connect trading partners electronically and decentralize the trading environment in profound and positive ways.

I stayed in Tribeca late into the evening, while Chris drew diagrams on his whiteboard and described to me his conception of the digital stock market of the future:

At its core was an electronic order book system very much like Instinet but accessible to anyone with a computer and a modem. As with Instinet, investors could post "limit" orders into this order book (i.e., orders to trade at a particular price). Or they could hit or take other posted orders by clicking on the price.

They could also use the limit order book to negotiate trades within the spreads. An investor might, for example, indicate interest in buying or selling a particular stock, disclose her name, set a price per share, and indicate the numbers of shares she wanted to trade. Or, she might simply disclose interest and not disclose anything else. Or she might disclose everything but her name. Whatever. And anybody seeing any of this information could negotiate with her right on-line.

And I do mean negotiate. Suppose you saw an offer by someone to sell a stock you were interested in at $15 ⅜. You knew the spread was $15 to $16. You might just open up a dialogue—like going into a chat room on the Internet to discuss trading the stock at $15 ⁵⁄₁₆.

Even more radically, Chris also outlined a novel plan for using the Global Trade system to go beyond limit-order trading for price improvement in trading market orders. Here's how it would work:

Suppose a retail investor wants to sell 1,000 shares of Terminal Technology. She does not know or care about the price she sells at. She just wants to sell at the market price. But she wants to sell now.

The stock trades on the NASDAQ dealer market. In the traditional system, the investor's broker would route her order to a market maker, and the trade would be executed immediately at the market price. If the quote on the stock were a bid price of $32.00 and an ask price of $32.50, the investor gets it done at $32.00.

In Chris's system, by contrast, the broker would broadcast that order to sell 1,000 shares over the Internet, together with a real-time quote showing the market price. This would set up an immediate auction. Anyone out there, anyone logging on to the Internet from anywhere at all, could consider the sell order and the market maker's quote, and then could choose to enter a competitive bid. If the competitive bid was better than the price offered by the market maker, that would take the trade away from the market maker. If no competitive bid emerged from the auction, then the order would immediately get passed on to the market maker to be traded at the spread. The total transaction—order, broadcast, auction, bidding—would take place within seconds. It was nothing less than an open, national auction for every retail market order.

By the end of the evening, Chris and I had a deal in principle. Although the details would take some time to work out, we had joined forces to create the digital stock market. We would use the software of the failed Chicago Match and the technology of the Internet, not to mention Chris's unique command of the markets and automation, to expand electronic trading beyond institutions only, and beyond traditional limit-order trading from an electronic order book.

As part of the deal, Chris agreed to sell Wit Capital his electronic trading software system in exchange for stock. He agreed to join Wit Capital and to bring with him Walter Buist, another veteran of stock exchange and brokerage automation, and eight other indispensable Global Trade staff members as the Wit Capital development team. In one fell swoop, Wit Capital had obtained the powerful software that would become its essential operational tool and more than doubled its staff size.

15.

You Can't Trade without Orders

One thing you certainly need to build a business is a way to distribute and deliver your product. In the case of Wit Capital, that meant both the technology mechanism and the securities industry players who might participate in the services Wit Capital wanted to provide. Walter Buist took on the technical task. And while his programmers went to work developing an Internet front end through which customers might access our electronic trading system, Chris and I took on the task of searching out participants. We wanted to test the two key premises underlying Chris's plan to create the digital stock market:

First, that there were trading professionals outside the market-making community who would welcome the opportunity to provide liquidity in national auctions for retail order flow—and thus compete with the market makers.

Second, that once we had demonstrated the significant savings that could accrue to investors by routing orders through our trading system, retail stock brokerage firms would welcome the opportunity to send their customers' orders to us.

We validated the first premise quickly and easily. Chris's instincts about the professional trading community had been right on. Call after call confirmed that a variety of trading firms were eager for an opportunity to compete against market makers for access to retail market orders. A number of them, in fact, indicated early on that they would gladly build computer-to-computer interfaces to our system if we could get them a steady stream of retail order flow.

Computer model traders were particularly pleased at the idea of going up against the market makers. Highly automated, these firms had mastered algorithmic trading strategies that enabled them to exploit market inefficiencies in ways less technologically astute firms could not hope to do. As a result, the market-making firms persistently tried to avoid taking orders from these firms, which left the firms vulnerable to market-maker competition. The prospect of an open system in which they could regularly bid against the market prices set by the market makers was an exciting one.

Also excited about participating in our digital stock market were options traders who worked at the Chicago Options Exchange. On the floor of the exchange, Chris and I were entertained by John Najarian, the head of Mercury Trading, a successful options market maker.

A colorful and engaging character who had once played linebacker for the Chicago Bears—and now sports a stylish ponytail—John showed us how options traders, as a hedging strategy, regularly trade the common stocks that underlie their options positions. As with the computer model traders, however, traditional market-making firms don't want to trade with the options traders. They find the options traders intimidating, smart enough to move markets with their trades. The only remaining option for the options traders, therefore, is to find access from the floor of the exchange to equity trades. And the only reliable access is through the Instinet terminals that are maintained in their offices and staffed with speed typists. Offer these traders the possibility of access to electronic trading on their own PC screens right on the floor of the exchange, as we did, and you will be very well received, as we were. The message from the options traders was loud and clear: Get us access to orders from brokers, and we will give better prices than the market makers—just to have the opportunity to get the executions.

John Najarian was so excited at the prospect of the digital stock market, in fact, that he offered to become a director of Wit Capital and invest in the development of the system. He also offered to help Chris and me solicit the participation of other options traders.

But if the world was full of frustrated traders more than willing to offer retail investors better prices for their trades than were quoted by market makers, the brokerage community offered a very different response. Brokers had not the slightest interest in routing their orders to our new trading system. They had not the slightest interest in a system that promised better prices for investors. The reasons became obvious the more I learned about the brokerage industry. I learned, for example, about the many paths to broker profits built into the existing brokerage system. I learned how the industry had carefully shrouded its system in layers of deliberate complexity that kept the investing public in the dark. I learned that much of the prosperity brokerage firms enjoy comes at the expense of the customer. Without a single exception that I could find, brokerage firms invariably profit from the wide spreads at which the trades are executed on the traditional markets.

How? In addition to commissions, brokers earn a little something extra when they route customer orders to market makers or specialists. The market makers pay what is called payment for order flow, or order flow remuneration—a percentage of the profit the market maker has made in the trade. Call it an incentive payment from the specialist or market maker, something that keeps the broker sending the order flow their way. Or, call it by its rightful name: a kickback. The specialist or market maker is willing to pay it in exchange for the opportunity to trade against the order at an artificially wide spread.

For example, suppose Joe Smith orders his broker—we'll call her Betty—to sell 1,000 shares of ABC Corporation. There's a range of market makers to whom Betty might take the sell order. Fred is one of those market makers. He can buy ABC stock at $10 per share and sell it at $10.25 per share, thus making a quarter-per-share spread on the order. Obviously, Fred wants as many orders to trade ABC stock as he can possibly get. It makes sense, therefore, to offer Betty 2 cents per share in payment for her customers' order flow. Fred still makes 23 cents per share on the deal, so he comes out ahead. And so does Betty. In fact, the bottom line of this practice—which has been challenged in court and found perfectly legal—is that your broker, the agent you have hired to work on your behalf, is not necessarily getting you the best trade possible. He is not necessarily even looking for the best trade possible. He is looking for the market maker who will give him the best return possible. In fact, your broker's share of the market maker's profit is more important to him than the commission he gets from you.

In the meantime, you the investor are not getting what you paid for, i.e., a loyal agent dedicated to finding you the best possible execution at the best possible price. You're getting less.

You would think order flow payments would be illegal. I did. How could a broker get away with selling his customers' orders? Didn't he have the fiduciary duty to get the customer the best price possible? How could he get a kickback for selecting one market maker over another, or over a competing execution service?

But when I went to the law library back at Cravath and did some research, I found that order flow payments had been sanctioned by the courts and even embraced by the SEC regulators.

It is an open secret that order flow payments are pervasive in the brokerage industry, and it was obvious as I went from brokerage firm to brokerage firm that the brokers had no intention of giving them up no matter how bad they were for customers.

Here's a challenge to every reader of this book: Ask your broker if he takes payment for order flow. The fact is, he may do so without even knowing he does so, without even understanding how the system works. Check the fine print of your brokerage contract. By law, it must now disclose that it takes payment for order flow. But while failure to disclose is illegal, taking the payment is not.

The brokers we approached, and through Chris's contacts we had entrée to most of the industry's largest firms, quite naturally disapproved of our idea of the digital stock market. They more than disapproved; they scorned it. It was naïve and ill-conceived, they said, to expect brokers to forgo that sizable portion of their revenue represented by order flow payments just so they could get their customers better prices! Even the discount brokers, renowned for having aggressively advanced the interests of their customers over the business-as-usual procedures of the large full-service brokerage firms, laughed at our proposition. Put the interests of customers above the few pennies per share they earned by selling their order flow? Nonsense.

No wonder we ran into a wall at the borders of the brokerage community. We'd get a meeting at yet another firm, demonstrate our formidable technology, describe our plans for the digital stock market, and wait for the invariable question: What happens to order flow payments? Then, when they heard the answer, we waited for the invariable response to our proposal: No.

So we gave up on the notion of serving retail brokers with our digital stock market. Instead, we would have to create our own brokerage firm. We would have to build a direct relationship to each and every individual investor, then use the Global Trade system to let our customers trade among themselves in the new marketplace.

This effort, however, was going to take a bigger team, more technology, and even more capital.

16.

A Royal Fourth of July

In the midst of all this activity, I was invited by *Upside* magazine to participate in a panel session on "IPOs and Capital Formation on the Internet." The panel was to be held at the end of June in Palo Alto, the heart of California's technology community and of its venture capital community. It's also the home of *Upside*, which is one of the bibles for both those communities, reporting on emerging technologies, up-and-coming technology companies, and venture capital activities. *Upside* had voted me among the hundred most influential people in technology for what we had achieved with Wit-Trade, although I think I was number ninety-six. So I flew out to Palo Alto to join SEC Commissioner Wallman, a professor at Stanford Law School, and representatives from a number of brokerage firms at the Hyatt Rickeys in Palo Alto.

The panel session convened at seven-thirty in the morning, and the room was packed. There were at least four hundred people there, and among them were some of the nation's most exciting technology entrepreneurs. As the speakers began, it became clear that Wit Capital was something of a lightning rod for the discussion. Commissioner Wallman, for one, was extremely supportive of what we were doing, and he said so in no uncertain terms. The brokers, however, were less convinced. The representative from Montgomery Securities, its general counsel, was particularly dismissive of Wit Capital. It was naïve, he told the audience, to believe that individual investors did not have access to IPOs. It was foolish, he went on to say, to assert that investment banks colluded with the big institutional investment funds to sell IPO stocks to a discrete, exclusive group of investors. In short, he claimed, the very ground on which Wit Capital stood was shaky, while the stated aim of Wit Capital was nothing short of outrageous.

Then it was my turn. I faced my audience. "How many of you consider yourselves in some sense individual investors?" I asked. All but a few hands were raised in answer. "And how many of you," I went on to query, "have ever been invited to a road show for an initial public offering?" Not a single hand went up. No one in the audience had ever been near a road show. The people in this audience were savvy business people, savvy technologists, and savvy investors. They knew both the possibilities of technology and the reality of what happens when an IPO stock is issued. "How many of you," I asked in a final question, "would like to be able to buy IPO stock at the offering price?" The entire audience, four hundred strong, raised their hands en masse. My point was made.

One of the members of the audience that day was a Middle East–born Stanford Ph.D. who had created and then sold his own computer company and was now a venture capitalist. After the session, he introduced himself to me and asked if I had a few minutes to talk to him. We went to lunch, where he told me he represented a "substantial" investor on whose behalf he was now seeking out up-and-coming technology companies. Could he come see our operation in New York? By all means, I answered.

I returned to New York, and shortly thereafter the doctor duly showed up. He met David and Chris and Walter, and we showed him a demo of the Global Trade technology. That evening, he called me from a pay phone, reaching me at home at around eleven-thirty to ask if I would meet him at a coffee shop around the corner. There was an exciting air of mystery about it all—the unknown investor he represented, the late hour, the use of the pay phone. I went out and we met in the coffee shop. Two hours later, we had worked out a deal committing the investor to put about $1 million into Wit Capital.

The next morning, early, we met at the office and typed out a contract, finishing it up just before noon. We then hailed a cab and went uptown to the Waldorf Astoria Hotel, where I was going to meet my million-dollar investor. We took the elevator to a fourth-floor suite in the Waldorf Towers. "Andy," my new partner said, as I extended my hand to shake the hand of a distinguished-looking gentleman, "I would like you to meet His Highness—prince of the royal family."

After half an hour of pleasant chat, the prince sat back and lowered his gaze to the contract I had set on the table. I was motioned to sign the papers, which I did with the Bic pen that I had in my shirt pocket. I then slid the papers across the table to the prince. He flashed a meaningful look across the room to his trusted valet, who had stood silently since our arrival. The prince then suddenly, efficiently snapped his fingers, and the valet disappeared into the back private quarters. A moment later, he reappeared and approached the table. He handed the prince a pen, an expensive pen, a very private and personal pen, and the prince signed the papers, committing to invest $1 million in Wit Capital.

It was, appropriately, the Fourth of July—a time for celebration, a reason for fireworks.

17.

Filling In the Gaps

If we were going to build a full-fledged brokerage operation, David and I reasoned in the late summer of 1996, one of the first things we would need was someone who actually knew something about how a retail brokerage business operated. For a while, Chris and Walter could navigate through the technical challenges that lay ahead, and David and I remained reasonably confident we could guide the firm's overall direction, though none of us knew the first thing about running a brokerage business.

Two help-wanted ads in the *New York Times* bore no interesting fruit, nor did a large and more costly ad in the *Wall Street Journal*. A fortuitously placed call to our friends at Arthur Andersen, however, hit pay dirt. An alumna of the accountancy's brokerage practice just happened to be using the firm's contacts to network herself a new job. Our buddies at Arthur Andersen thought we might be interested and faxed us Julie Oliver's résumé.

We were very interested. It was the résumé of a woman who had worked for twelve years auditing retail brokerage firms for Arthur Andersen, had then become controller of a large broker dealer, and had gone to join Salomon Brothers as a senior accounting executive. But the bureaucracy and internal politics of the large financial services institution were getting her down—a familiar story to Wit Capital's staff—and Ms. Oliver thought that a young entrepreneurial firm on the cutting edge, like Wit Capital, would afford her the chance to broaden her responsibilities and grab an equity stake in the venture.

I suspect, however, that the sight of David and me in the beer company storage closet was not quite what Julie was expecting when she showed up for our first meeting. She wore her power blue Wall Street suit and carried an elegant leather briefcase full of skepticism. It was not your everyday job interview. Julie asked most of the questions. Over a period of two hours, that's a lot of questions.

I was thrilled: She was tough. She was direct. She was experienced. Clearly bright. Obviously able. Would she be crazy enough to give up her secure position at one of Wall Street's more prominent securities firms to join an out-of-work investment banker, a microbrewer, and an admittedly ruffled group of software developers? That's basically the only question I got to ask her at all. I put it to her just as the interview came to a close. Julie said she'd think about it.

The next day, I called Julie and invited her to come see us again. She said she was still thinking things over and wanted to do some research on both Spring Street Brewing and me. She also wanted to know something more about our prince.

About a week later, Julie called back for a second meeting. After three hours of further discussion, she agreed to join Wit Capital as our chief financial officer and de facto head of retail brokerage.

Now that we had finally found someone who could actually help design a brokerage business, we sat down to figure out how to build the business. Essentially, we decided that our opportunity lay in creating a fully automated electronic discount brokerage operation—where customers would interact with us through the Internet, through Touch-Tone telephone, and, someday, through the electronic services of the future. In short, they'd get through to us without having to go through human beings staffing telephone lines.

We were well aware, of course, that all around us, lots of new brokerage firms were likewise using the Internet and electronic trading. Through these technologies, they were lowering commissions while offering customers cost savings. They were also giving their customers unprecedented access to account information and to news and information services that helped form investment decisions. We decided that Wit Capital would also provide these low-cost brokerage services, news and information, research, and an array of other services and tools. But Wit would of course go farther than that. It would also offer access to such investment banking products as initial public offerings and venture capital investment opportunities, and it would also provide access to our digital stock market.

This was, in our view, a powerful offering from the marketing point of view: offering individual investors products and services historically available only to large institutions and the very wealthy was our wedge into the individual investor market. The more investors we could attract, the more we would win the business of raising capital from quality companies. The more capital raised, the more liquidity we could create between the spreads in the digital stock market. The more liquidity, the greater the lure for yet more new investors to join our community. And so on. Now all we had to do was find a technology we could integrate with Global Trade to carry out basic brokerage functions—opening accounts, routing orders to trade securities, keeping track of account balances.

At this point, Walter Buist, master technologist, made one of his many valuable contributions. If what we wanted was a straightforward electronic brokerage system, why not simply go to one of the firms that had already developed one and license it from them? Buy versus build. The classic business choice. To pursue it, we needed to find out who had such software and if they would sell it or rent it.

Walter and Chris went to work hunting through their network for vendors who trafficked in electronic brokerage software and came up empty-handed. It turns out there weren't any traditional securities firms yet interested in electronic Internet trading.

So I picked up the telephone and called the heads of three early-stage firms that were already operating electronic trading through the Internet: E-Trade Securities, Lombard, and AmeriTrade. I had heard from all three back when we held the initial public offering of Spring Street Brewing. Now, all three enthusiastically volunteered to join our venture by licensing their front-end software. Walter and I left New York to explore these intriguing possibilities.

Our first stop was Omaha, Nebraska, where a crafty entrepreneur named Joe Ricketts was operating four distinct discount brokerages—with four different brand names but all under the AmeriTrade umbrella—out of a huge compound near Warren Buffet's home office.

Joe's system, however, didn't go far enough for Wit Capital. There seemed no way to make it the basis for building customer account data, routing trade orders to an electronic stock market, or handling the digital stock market.

We flew next to the San Francisco offices of Lombard Institutional Brokerage. Here too, however, we were disappointed to learn the technology in this operation was not up to our needs. In fact, although Lombard's customers could transmit orders through the Internet, once the orders arrived at Lombard's offices, more often than not they were printed at a local printer, and their information was then reentered by clerks into an old-fashioned terminal connected to the clearing firm's mainframe computer. There was no way we could build our stock market of the future on Lombard's modest technology.

From Lombard, we traveled down the coast to E-Trade Securities just outside Palo Alto. Although not the first, E-Trade was quickly becoming the leading on-line discount brokerage firm and had just been backed by General Atlantic, an East Coast venture capital firm. It was an obvious contender to capture the first-to-market advantage as it rolled out ambitious investing tools.

For our tour of the facility, E-Trade packed their conference room with top executives, even bringing in founder and chairman Bill Porter. In the end, however, it was clear that E-Trade had not developed any more technology than Joe Ricketts. There was no way we could base our trading market on a system that just transmitted traditional orders to the same old back-end execution and clearing system. E-Trade, Lombard, AmeriTrade: that is all any of them could offer.

But while we were running out of options in sunny California, Julie and David were coming up winners back in New York.

As usually happens, the winning ticket came through networking—in this case, from one fellow who knew another fellow. One of the projects Julie had assigned herself was to build a relationship for Wit Capital with a clearing firm that would extend credit to all of our customers and handle what's called the back office—all the custodial and administrative aspects of the brokerage business. After meeting with each of the leading providers of such services, we had settled on U.S. Clearing Corporation, a subsidiary of the Quick & Reilly Group, and, with some 320 brokerage firm clients, the second-largest provider of such services in the retail brokerage industry. In the course of her discussions with U.S. Clearing, Julie mentioned that Walter and I were out on the Coast chasing down electronic brokerages, and someone on the staff suggested that we contact a guy named David Kingland, who had founded a company called the Kingland Corporation in Mason City, Iowa.

After a brief introductory conference call with Kingland seemed promising, Walter and I headed for Iowa, and this time we were not disappointed. Unlike the superficial pass through systems that had been developed by the first wave of Internet trading systems, the Kingland product was a full-blown brokerage—the database and processing software that could support the entire operation of an automated brokerage firm.

Of course, Kingland's system had never been designed with the Internet in mind. On the contrary. It had been built for Bank of America to support basic brokerage operations. Its purpose was to assist human brokers in tracing and managing their customers' accounts through powerful account maintenance and order routing and tracking modules. Our plan was to adapt the Kingland system to do more.

We would make it function through a new interface that would connect investors directly with their accounts through the Internet. We would expand its functionality so that customers could actually fill out their account applications on-line, without giving the information to a brokerage officer who then scrawls it illegibly on a paper application. We would integrate the system with the matching engines of the Global Trade system to support the digital stock market. Finally, we would make it possible to route orders for new stock offerings to an electronic order book.

We were confident all these modifications were doable. So was Dave Kingland. We negotiated a license arrangement, and then we quickly set to work to enhance the system. It would, after all, be the launching pad from which Wit Capital would blast off.

18.

Raining Angels

While Walter and his team worked through the early winter months with Kingland's crew, integrating brokerage and trading, I was having great luck and success filling gaps in our management ranks and raising the capital we needed to launch our new venture. In both cases, Wit's media fame paid out important dividends.

One day in January 1997, for example, a young man named Mark Boyce arrived at our offices. He wanted to know, he said, exactly what we were up to. Mark had an M.B.A. from Harvard, experience as a marketing executive at Microsoft—back when Bill Gates commanded a mere two thousand employees—and a background as an investment banker. Up until the previous year, he had worked at Lotus, first as head of business development, then, after IBM acquired the company, in charge of developing IBM's Internet strategy.

Since leaving Lotus, Mark had been working on his own as a consultant and business development strategist for young Internet start-ups, which is why he had been intrigued by what he had read about Wit Capital. He wondered whether we might be able to help any of his clients raise capital in innovative ways that played to their strengths as Internet companies.

After just a brief conversation, I wondered if he would like to join

Wit Capital and bring to it the relationships he was already developing. Mark Boyce thus became cohead of investment banking.

Another talented and experienced person wandered our way around that same time. His name was Bruce Foerster, and he was a veteran of more than fifteen hundred IPOs. Bruce had been head of capital markets at Lehman Brothers before he retired and moved to South Beach, Florida, to start a small consultancy. Intrigued by what we were doing, however, he offered to help us build both an investment banking strategy and strong relationships with mainstream investment banks. Our team was getting stronger and stronger.

And in addition to Bruce, I met Robert Griggs, at an Internet trade show in Manhattan, and knew within hours that I'd like him on our team. Robert had already been a successful technology entrepreneur—twice. First, he cofounded a software company that ultimately merged with another firm to create Macromedia. More recently, he founded the world's first Internet-only radio channel, Net Radio, which he had just sold to a large record-distribution company. Although based in Minneapolis, Robert quickly offered to join Wit Capital and relocate to New York to become head of Wit Capital's business development.

We were almost as lucky finding funding as we had been finding talented people. Around Christmastime 1996, we prepared a second private placement memorandum for $5.5 million and circulated it to prospective venture capital and angel investors.

Relying on introductions from our initial investor group, as well as on the connections that Bruce Foerster and Robert Griggs brought with them, we were given a hearing by an amazing group of would-be backers. Not everyone was a buyer, of course, but we did manage to attract a fantastic group of supporters.

Ronald Readmond, for example, who had been the vice chairman of Charles Schwab and before that a partner at Alex, Brown, agreed to make a sizable investment—and to join our board of directors. Ron in turn introduced me to a legendary venture capital investor named Frank Bonsal, who had been a founding partner of New Enterprise Associates, one of the largest high-technology venture capital firms in the country. After a few meetings and some preliminary background checks, Mr. Bonsal too agreed to become an investor.

Through Bruce Foerster, I had an introduction to John Gutfreund, the former chairman of Salomon Brothers, who also agreed to become a shareholder in Wit Capital. Bruce also introduced me to John Herzog and Buzzy Geduld, founding principals of the market-making firm Herzog, Heine & Geduld. They both invested in us, too.

An odd twist of coincidence led me to another of our investors—or rather, led him to us. One day in March the telephone rang and a man who said his name was Weeden announced that he was looking for Andy Klein—the guy behind Wit Capital and Spring Street Brewing.

Don Weeden was heir to a century-old brokerage firm, Weeden & Company, that had been started by his father. In the seventies, Weeden & Company had been an early backer of Jerry Pustilnik's Instinet, and when that business was faltering, Don Weeden had invested further, at one time owning more than 80 percent of Instinet equity. So, when Bill Lupien turned Instinet around and ultimately arranged its sale to Reuters, Weeden did very well indeed. Weeden had read about Wit Capital in the press and had been very intrigued, but that wasn't why he was calling. He was calling because years earlier he had known an Andy Klein who had worked at the SEC. He thought that Andy Klein was the guy behind Wit Capital and he was trying to get in touch with his old friend. I was the wrong Andy Klein, of course, but Don Weeden nevertheless agreed to meet with me at his office in Connecticut. And he and a group of affiliated investors ultimately became major investors in Wit Capital.

One of our most formidable and most important investors came to us via Robert Griggs. Ron Conway had invested in Robert's software company years earlier, in Robert's Silicon Valley days. "He's the ultimate angel investor," Robert said of Ron. "If you can interest him in your efforts, you can count on him for invaluable support and strategic help."

Boy, was he right about that.

Thanks to Robert's introduction, Ron Conway agreed to meet with me at a restaurant in San Francisco. Fortunately, he was intrigued with our plans for Wit Capital. But for the moment, "intrigued" was all he was. Over the course of the next week or so, however, Ron conducted an extensive due-diligence review of Wit Capital. He phoned me every day—sometimes several times a day. He sent a technologist to explore our software and to probe Walter and the Kingland developers. He also sent a former investment banker to check us out.

After this rather rigorous vetting of our business, Ron invited me to dine again in San Francisco. He had an offer for me, he said, but first he thought he owed me a word of explanation.

The scrupulous and laborious diligence was only partly for his own purposes. Rather, he explained, he was a member of an elite group of Silicon Valley investors known locally as the "Band of Angels." There were fifty investors in the Band. Each had been a successful technology entrepreneur. All were interested in investing in promising young technology companies. As the Band of Angels, they did so collectively. Each month, the Band would meet to review two or three companies. Each company chosen for review had to be sponsored by a member of the Band of Angels who had performed due diligence and had personally committed to invest in the company. Ron offered to invest personally in Wit Capital and to sponsor our appearance before the group at their next monthly dinner.

The rules of the dinner were as rigorous as the rules of sponsorship. I was given ten minutes—no more—to make my case. My audience included a former top manager of Intel, the former CFO of Intuit, the founder of the Silicon Valley Bank, and dozens of men and women I had never heard of who had nevertheless sold companies for hundreds of millions of dollars.

I guess my ten minutes were engaging. Within just a few days investments from the Band of Angels had exceeded another million dollars.

Through the spring and into summer, we finalized our launch plans, refined our strategy, and added the final touches to our management team by hiring a head of retail brokerage and a marketing director. We also managed to keep our name in the papers. Our story continued to engross the technology press and the business press in equal measure:

"A little beer maker has new plans that could drive Wall Street to drink," said the Associated Press.

"Andrew Klein has created an Internet version of Wall Street," trumpeted *Internet World*.

"Will the Web morph into a stock exchange?" wondered *Net Magazine*.

"The Web is rapidly refashioning the way the brokerage industry does business," wrote the *Wall Street Journal*, and it asked, "Where are [Klein] and others in the online brokerage business heading?"

I was about to answer that question.

19.

A Pause to Refresh

Wit Capital was conceived as the world's first investment bank and brokerage firm dedicated to offering and trading securities through the Internet and the World Wide Web. It is aimed at nothing less than revolutionizing the process of capital formation and stock trading by giving retail investors the same opportunities for direct participation in the process that has traditionally been enjoyed by institutional investors and wealthy individuals. As it turns out, that revolution is something of a return to the future.

Go back to the early days of our nation's history, to the thriving commercial port of New York, where securities were bought and sold like commodities, no different from the bales of cotton and casks of sugar waiting on the docks. Most of the bidding for securities took place under a buttonwood tree on lower Wall Street or, in cold weather, in front of the fire at the Tontine Coffee House on the corner of Wall and Water Streets. There, traders bought and sold stocks at auction through competitive bidding.

Then one day in May 1792, twenty-four brokers and merchants decided they would be better off if they agreed to trade only with one another, to avoid public auctions, and to collect commissions on all sales of public stock. The Buttonwood Agreement, as it was called, was the start of the New York Stock Exchange, and it was the first strike for exclusivity in what had been a vibrantly open street market.

Stockbrokers now became the way station between companies looking for capital and people with money to invest. Similarly, such brokers became indispensable to the secondary market trading of securities.

As the market evolved down the decades and the number of investors grew, so did the number of stockbrokers, until the whole process had become downright unmanageable.

In the boom years that followed World War II, a single high-powered brokerage might have fifteen thousand retail stockbrokers: fifteen thousand people competing against one another for stock being issued and for customers to sell it to. Veterans of the Pacific campaign were reminded of jungle warfare.

Issuing companies and their underwriters, seeking some order in all this chaos, found it a good deal easier to court a few large institutional investors—insurance companies, pension plans, institutional money managers—rather than try to manage the thousands of retail distributors.

The shift of focus, however, from lots of retail investors to a few wholesale investors, also meant that the large investment banks could increasingly dominate the market—by allocating supply and thus affecting demand.

The eventual result of all these natural evolutionary processes was a good example of what today might be called leverage: a limited number of powerful investment banks hand in glove with a limited number of huge institutional investors who basically decided which companies' stocks got the chance for liquidity and which brokers got to do the trading. This is that very exclusive club I described at the start of this book.

The club works. Everyone in it can count on a particular benefit—which is why everyone in it wants things to stay just as they are.

Comes now a new technology that enables creative entrepreneurial firms—firms like Wit Capital—to challenge the exclusivity of this club. It's a technology that came about by happenstance, and no one is yet precisely sure how it will affect our lives—beyond predicting that its impact will be profound and fundamental. It's the Internet, of course, and it's worth reviewing briefly just what it is and does.

As people sometimes forget, the Internet started in 1969 as a government-funded research project connecting major university computers. The Cold War was raging at the time, and the government wanted a communications network that would continue to work even if some sites were destroyed by nuclear attack. Researchers believed that by networking computers, then connecting the networks, data traffic could find alternate routes should the most direct route be shut down.

This was strictly a matter for engineers and scientists. There were no home computers in 1969, there were relatively few in the business world, and what computers there were were big, complex, and not at all user-friendly. Even the engineers and scientists who were the early users of the original Internet had to master complex procedures to move around in it.

Over the years, however, technological developments opened the network to nontechnical people, who in turn began to find all sorts of new ways for the network to develop. Mostly because of their ability to communicate with one another, users began sending things to one another, sharing resources, transmitting information—first in bits and bytes, then in files. Businesses began to use the network, first as an internal communications tool connecting their own networks, then as a way to reach customers, even to sell products. Resources were added to the network, tools were developed to index the resources, mechanisms evolved for searching the indexes, and techniques were born to link index to index. New standards, or communications protocols, made it possible for otherwise incompatible sets of resources to "talk to" one another, until there was a network of networks that was worldwide and offered a vast range of services of every conceivable kind.

In 1989, a particularly important technology breakthrough introduced a new protocol that embraced all the varied communications procedures and standards that had developed over time. This protocol was based on hypertext—a system of embedding links in text—and it eventually became known as the World Wide Web, one of the fastest-growing technologies in computing history.

Today, the Internet comprises thousands of regional networks around the world. On any given day, it connects roughly twenty million users in more than fifty countries—a global community of users accustomed to having direct access to information, services, and one another. The vast majority of these users are between the ages of twenty-one and thirty, and nearly half are professionals. None of them needs to understand the underlying technologies, although many do, in order to navigate from location to location, to search out information, to communicate with one another via E-mail or user-groups or chat rooms.

Nobody owns the Internet; no single governing body controls its use. Time and again, Internet users have shown that they favor open access and that they prize equal access. It is fair to say that they have little patience with middlemen, or with any kind of fire wall that separates them from what they're after on the Net.

As we are constantly being told, the Internet is going to change forever the way people create, access, and absorb information, and that, in turn, will change the way we learn, study, communicate, shop, bank, are entertained, are governed, do business, invest.

Through Wit Capital Corporation, I am using the Internet to try to change investment banking and the way stocks are traded. Both need changing.

20.

A Technical Rewrite of
the Investment Banking Primer
PART 1: THE IPO

There's no law that says you have to use a traditional investment bank when you're trying to raise money for your company. Yet Wall Street investment bankers have made themselves the sine qua non of the capital formation process. Just about every path corporate America can take to needed cash goes through their plushly carpeted offices. If you're a business looking for substantial financial wherewithal, it is axiomatic that you put yourself in the hands of one of the colossal investment banks.

Not anymore. At least, not necessarily.

Today, computer and telecommunications technology challenge the need for offices—even plushly carpeted ones—when all you want to do is invest or be invested in.

Taking advantage of the technology, new electronic firms such as Wit Capital—call them digital investment banks—offer alternative versions to the ways of raising money that old-line investment banks have devised. Less expensive alternatives. More efficient alternatives. Alternatives that subvert the exclusivity of the private investment banking club and open wide its doors.

At the heart of the capital formation process is the IPO—the initial public offering of stock by a privately held company that is going public, that is going to begin trading on a national stock market.

As American as apple pie, the IPO is now being exported, along with American-style capitalism, throughout the global economy. Even at home, the number of IPOs per year continues to rise steadily, as it has done for some years, thanks in particular to a law passed in 1974 and to a trend that shows no sign of lessening. The law is ERISA, the Employee Retirement Income Security Act, which made it legal to invest retirement pension money in equities. Before ERISA, bonds, considered less risky than securities, had been the traditional pension investment. Since ERISA, institutional investor participation in the stock market has increased dramatically, and pension fund investments in stocks have swelled from a trickle to a flood.

Helping to keep the floodgates open is the trend toward 401(k) plans and their corollaries—Keogh plans, IRAs, SEPs, and the like. Thanks to 401(k)-style investing, Americans have been putting their money into stocks every time they get a paycheck. In fact, for the most part, the money is automatically deducted from paychecks and invested in the stock or fund of the employee's choice. Thus 401(k) investing has become a veritable wellspring of cash for the stock market, and companies looking to grow just love to drink in its waters.

There are other factors encouraging new issues of stock—for example, falling interest rates that make the stock market particularly attractive to investors, and the rising recognition, on the part of the baby boomers, that they will one day retire and had better find some good stocks to invest in now.

The bottom line is that the equity market keeps getting bigger and bigger, making it the place to go when you need to raise capital. That is why there are more and more and more IPOs each year. In 1974, for example, Wall Street did a total of eight IPOs. In the bull market of the 1990s, eight per week would not be considered abnormal.

Step one in the typical, traditional IPO is when the issuing company chooses an investment bank to underwrite the offering. Issuer and underwriter then determine how much capital should be raised, the type of security to be issued, the price of the security, the cost to the issuer, the cut for the investment bank, and other details. Once an agreement in principle is reached, the investment bank is ready to go out and solicit orders for the company's securities.

Their first stop is the big institutional funds. That's logical. After all, it's the big institutions that have the cash resources not only to purchase large blocks of securities in the first place, but also to purchase more of the stock in the critical period immediately following the deal going public. During that period, when the unseasoned securities first hit the public market, it is useful to have some cash reserves handy in case the stock issue needs propping up. So the investment bankers quite naturally look first to the big institutional investors—say, ten or fifteen of the major hedge funds and large money managers—hoping to give this untested enterprise, the company going public, the strongest possible head start.

Secondarily, they'll allocate a portion of the stock issue to retail investors. Very rich retail investors. Loyal retail investors. Good customers who can be counted on to generate consistently large fees on the retail brokerage side of the firm's business.

Between the limited number of institutional investors and the narrow selection of wealthy individuals, the supply of stock in the IPO has already been circumscribed. At the same time, the investment bankers are out promoting the new-issue stock to a whole network of retail brokers, promoting the stock to the brokers so the brokers will promote the stock to their individual investor and smaller institutional investor customers. Since IPOs carry a hot and sexy cachet—and provide a good reason for your broker to suggest some commission-generating movement in your account—brokers need little encouragement from the investment bankers to push an IPO stock. "Here it comes," the investment bankers tell the brokers, who tell their customers, "The next hot stock is in the pipeline. The next Netscape, or Boston Beer Company, or Snapple is on its way. Get ready."

As individual investors get the phone calls from their brokers, they rub their hands together with delight, and they get ready for the next hot company to go public.

That is just what the investment bankers want: widespread interest in stocks whose issue they virtually control. When supply is limited and demand is expansive, the chances are good that the price will appreciate as soon as the stock hits the market. For the retail investors, it means that while they will not have the opportunity to buy the stock at the low offering price granted big institutions and wealthy individuals, they are counted on to trade up the stock price in the after-market.

In addition, the investment bankers will typically underprice the IPO stock. On the one hand, that's understandable: the stock is an unknown quantity. Suppose the issuing company is a Web search engine company, and suppose it's the fifteenth Web search engine company trading stock on the exchange. To distinguish it from the other Web search engine companies—the fourteen so-called comparables—and attract buyers, it makes sense to discount the stock. Institutional investors look on this discount as the premium they're offered for participating in the process to begin with.

On the other hand, management of the issuing company may look on the discount as a betrayal—as money left on the table.

If the issuing company managers rant and rave that the discount price undervalues their company, and they very often do, the usual result is hoarse company managers. There's really no alternative to dealing with the major investment banks; if they say "Discount or die," the invariable result is discount.

Underpriced, overhyped, its supply closely guarded by a limited number of institutional and very rich investors, the IPO stock hits the public market. The retail buyers are ready, expectant, hopeful. As soon as they hear from their brokers, they buy. The institutional and wealthy individual investors looking for a quick and decisive profit get ready to flip the stock. They hold it for an hour, or maybe a couple of days, even a week or two. Then they sell. This is why they have bought the stock in the first place: to sell it fast. In fact, there are some funds that exist solely to get in on this flipping: they make their killing in the early price appreciation—the average new issue trades up nearly 20 percent in the first hour of trading—and then they get out.

Meanwhile, the individual investors have moved in, buying up the stock and bidding up its price. They buy and buy, and the price rises and rises—until there's little demand left for the stock, and the price of course goes down. Depending on timing, here is where individual retail investors may lose a lot of money or, at best, just about hold on to the value they believed they were purchasing.

Of course, some retail investors do make money. The reality, however, is that the IPO has been orchestrated for the benefit of the investment bankers who are collecting huge fees on the deal, and for the benefit of the institutional investors who get preferred access and a preferred price on the stock. As for individual retail investors, the IPO deck is stacked against them.

That isn't competitive carping on my part. *Individual Investor* magazine, the bible of the individual investor community, made it official in 1996 when it stopped reporting on imminent IPOs. The reason? The magazine's editors asserted that it would be "inappropriate" to continue covering IPOs since the magazine's subscribers, those 350,000 individuals interested in buying stocks, were never able to buy quality IPOs at anything close to the offering price.

In a May 1997 story, *II*'s Andrew Feinberg reported: "Getting a piece of a hot IPO is pure quid pro quo. So if you're not already a client of a full-service broker, it's crazy to switch to one just to get occasional scraps of good deals, unless you're really desperate for something to talk about at cocktail parties. You'll almost invariably pay thousands more in commissions on less sexy trades to get those 'free' IPO profits." I could not have said it better myself.

Wit Capital is changing this. Wit Capital—and the other investment banks that will invariably spring up on the Internet—are changing the IPO procedure and the IPO market. Whether we're lead-managing an IPO for a company, or acting as a distributing participant in another investment bank's IPO, we're opening the process to individuals, offering smaller pieces of equity and letting retail investors participate directly in the IPO on an equal footing with institutions. Over time, I believe that will defuse the all-pervasive clout of the investment banks and institutional investors. It will break the hammerlock they have exercised over the price of IPO stock and over who gets to invest in it.

At the same time, we're making the IPO process far less expensive than it has traditionally been. The Wit Capital way of doing an IPO does not incur the exorbitant costs of printing and transmitting prospectuses and other documentation. We do not use brokers, who must be paid commissions. Instead, we use the Internet, and that makes all the difference. Here's how it works:

A company wishing to issue stock still comes to an investment banker, only now it comes to an electronic investment banker like Wit Capital. "Electronic" describes the medium through which we link up with customers and other participants in the process. Just like any traditional investment bank, Wit Capital has all the professional capabilities to handle due diligence, to participate in valuation, to structure a deal, to prepare all offering materials, and to navigate through the regulatory process. Once the offering is ready to be marketed, however, the traditional road shows open only to large institutions will have no part in the process. Rather, once we announce an IPO, those who are interested can log on to our Web site and see the prospectus, take a video tour of the company, hear and see audiovisual statements by the company's managers. No one gets a sneak preview of the information before anyone else; no one has access to more information than anyone else. It's strictly "first come, first served." The technology doesn't care who you are or how big an investor; it is value-neutral.

The investor who wants to buy into the IPO then clicks a button on the screen to put in a buy order. Again, the rule is "first come, first served." The technology tags each order as it comes in, queuing would-be shareholders in order and noting the price each is offering. The prospectus has set down what is called a red-herring price for the stock—a preliminary range of prices aimed primarily at eliciting a response. For example, the issuer and the underwriter may think they can sell the stock for between $10 and $12 per share, and that's the red-herring price the prospectus will announce. The response to that range will quickly become evident in the buy orders that come in from prospective investors—either limit orders, where purchasers set a price above which they will not buy, or market orders, where purchasers agree to buy at whatever price. As the order book fills up, it becomes a reflection of the market's expectations for the IPO stock— a useful tool for underwriter and issuer as they evaluate demand and set a price for the stock.

The order book might show, for example, that there's substantial demand for the stock at $10, very little demand for it at $12, and varying levels of demand in between—enough, underwriter and issuer believe, that they could complete the transaction with an offering price of $10.50. This lets the law of supply and demand work within the discipline of the pricing mechanism to arrive at a price that is fairer to both the issuing company and the investor.

In any event, whatever the offering price, it is the same for everyone—retail investor and institutional investor alike. In fact, in the future, the offering price of an IPO stock might well be determined by auction—at least by an auction within a band of prices considered fair by the investment bank. Investors would be given a predetermined time frame during which they could bid on the price of a stock. At the end of the bidding period, the system would crunch an algorithm to determine the highest price that would clear the entire transaction. That would be the offering price. Everybody who bid at or above it would qualify for the IPO. Such an auction mechanism has the advantage of maximizing the price the company gets for its stock. In effect, the auction compresses into the preopening period the upward price bidding that typically occurs in the early aftermarket of an IPO, those first feverish days after the company goes public. With the upward bidding taking place before the stock hits the market, the company itself benefits if the stock appreciates.

Whether or not there is an unfettered auction to set the offering price, in a digitally distributed IPO there is a level playing field that gives the same price to everybody. By definition, that eliminates the flipping that tends to take place in a traditional IPO, replacing it with pure trading, the very thing for which stock markets were supposedly invented.

Obviously, individual investors benefit when a company goes public over the Internet. As Wit Capital vividly demonstrates, individual investors are entering the IPO process in droves—simply because they have been invited back and are being welcomed back.

The issuing companies also benefit. For one thing, they are getting the kinds of investors they want, the kinds who are going to hold on to their stock for the long term. The Internet enables a unique form of affinity marketing—that is, marketing securities to the people who are the logical buyers of those securities. When a company's prospectus is posted on the Internet rather than distributed narrowly by investment bankers and brokers, it has a far better chance of catching the eye of prospective investors who are interested in the company's product or service. Put the prospectus of a beer company on the Internet, for example, and you reach not just people interested in business, dabblers in the stock market, or investors looking for IPOs; you also reach beer drinkers, beer lovers, and lovers of beer drinkers—people who can identify with the company, people who want to advance the company's growth and contribute to its strength in every way possible. That's what happened when we sold Spring Street's shares. The people who bought the stock were people who drank Wit Beer. They were de facto supporters of the product in the marketplace. We thought it boded well for the future that they owned pieces of our company.

What's more, issuing companies get these highly desirable investors efficiently. A traditional IPO can cost hundreds of thousands of dollars in printing expenses alone. Prospectuses are printed. Letters are printed. Confirmations are printed. Add to this the cost—and bother—of transmitting all these documents, usually by courier, all across the country to the stock brokerage houses that are funneling the stock to individuals, to the institutions making their invest-ment decisions, and back and forth between issuing company and in-vestment bank.

Wit Capital's investment banking on the Internet is paperless. The prospectus is generated and filed with the SEC electronically, and it is electronically posted to a Web site. An E-mail announcing the IPO is then transmitted to the entire network of Wit Capital account hold-ers and prospective account holders, as well as the employees, suppli-ers, customers, and prospective customers of the company going public. Embedded in the E-mail is a hyperlink back to Wit Capital's Web site. All the recipient has to do is click on the hyperlink icon to be instantly routed to the prospectus. The cost saving is enormous.

Also saved is the cost of the road show presented by the issuing company executives and the investment bankers. Not just cost is saved here, but also time, energy, and outright angst. In the life of any company going through an IPO, the road show can prove a par-ticular headache. Just try getting a bunch of senior managers and in-vestment bankers on a plane to travel at great expense around the country—sometimes, around the world—so they can put on a show to sell themselves and their company to institutional investors. Over and over and over.

Still, a road show is necessary if the company is selling large chunks of its stock to a limited number of investors. If you're selling smaller pieces to a lot of individual investors, however, a road show is impossible—except digitally. Just put up a Web site. What is this company? What is its product? What do its offices look like? Let me tour the facilities, interview the chief financial officer, get a glimpse of the chief executive officer to test her mettle with my own eyes. Easy to do, and it doesn't cost a penny, on the World Wide Web.

For the issuing company, therefore, Wit Capital and similar Inter-net investment banks offer the best of both worlds: the investors they want to have at a price that makes the IPO process eminently cost-effective.

For the Internet investment banks like Wit Capital, which make their money by taking a percentage of the securities transaction, there are other benefits as well. We don't have to try to manage thousands and thousands of brokers. We don't have to travel the country trying to sell the IPO to huge institutions and funds. Technology has simplified our task and rationalized the process: one system, working on a rule of first come, first served, operated by a computer that cannot lie about who got there first.

Count the advantages of the digital IPO: For individual retail investors, an unprecedented opportunity to purchase public offering shares at fair offering prices—without having to pay commissions to a broker. For issuing companies, access to capital—and to desirable investors—at low cost. For the investment banks bringing investors and issuers together across the Internet, a technological solution to high costs and tedious activities. The only conceivable losers in the equation are the institutional investors, and I would argue that, in fact, they have a great deal to gain as well.

Let us assume, for example, a diminution of the relative leverage the big institutions now wield in the IPO process. That's a likely scenario; as the buying power of retail investors grows and grows, the big funds will be in less of a position to command terms, prices, and attention. One possible response might be to concentrate more intensely on their funds management task and on the active search for sound, intelligent investments. That is not a bad outcome. It's not bad for the people whose money the institutions manage, and it's not bad for the institutions, either.

Of course, IPOs are not the only means of capital formation. In fact, IPOs are invariably inappropriate for early-stage ventures; the pressures of managing a public market should not be visited upon a still unproven, untested concern. Rather, the IPO tends to be the last resort of fund-raising, the final booster thrust that puts the company into the orbit in which it will power itself. Before an entrepreneur ever gets to that point, he or she must seek venture capital for the enterprise.

21.

A Technical Rewrite of
the Investment Banking Primer
PART 2: VENTURE CAPITAL

The term "venture capital" embraces both the institutional venture capital firms and private placement financing. It's what the early-stage enterprise is looking for to stay afloat until it can develop its product, or create its market, or find its niche. The term implies both hazard and daring, and this is accurate: the investment carries a high degree of risk along with a high degree of potential reward. As with IPOs, such investments have historically been the sole property of institutions and the very rich. Individuals have rarely had access to investment in early-stage enterprises. And as with IPOs, Wit Capital is planning to change that.

The typical venture capital firm today is a partnership of perhaps six to eight professionals who have invested their own money and, in addition, are backed by such large institutional investors as insurance companies, pension plans, banks, and very wealthy individuals. It's up to the firm's partners, the professional managers, to invest the money on behalf of the fund. Typically, the investments are said to be "patient capital," the kind that might not yield a return for five or ten years. The partners are paid a percentage of the assets under their management, plus a share of the profits that the investments earn—strong motivation for them to find and cultivate the kinds of investments that will produce the greatest possible rewards.

That is why venture capital firms focus for the most part on enterprises they believe will become $300 million-a-year companies within three to five years. They want companies that will shift the paradigm of an industry and succeed explosively in the process.

Obviously, there aren't too many of those, and in their search for them, the venture capital firms often overlook or dismiss a lot of other promising companies. In my view, you haven't failed just because you haven't succeeded wildly all at once. A lot of companies that will not make $300 million in revenues in three years may still prove to be excellent growth opportunities over time.

In any event, once a venture capital firm has chosen a company to invest in, its help can be substantial. The firm's professional managers typically spend as much time nurturing the company as they did in selecting it in the first place. They involve themselves actively in advancing the company's growth, opening strategic doors, even helping choose the right managers. As likely as not, they will also demand a controlling interest in the company's affairs in return for their capital. Typically, that control will include the right to throw out the company's founders if things don't go well. Obviously, for entrepreneurs who have started a company, that is a high price to pay for the capital investment. But many simply have no choice.

There's another kind of venture capitalist known as the angel investor. Angel investors are essentially solo venture capitalists—very, very, very wealthy individuals who like to invest in early-stage companies. They like the risk; they like the potential reward—they typically accept an average of three deals for every ten considered, and they expect a 25-percent annual return—and they just simply enjoy the process. Like the professional managers of venture capital firms, angels will involve themselves in the life of the company in which they have invested. Many are highly successful business people who can lend their expertise and experience as well as their network of connections and their leadership example. They have become an increasingly important part of the venture capital picture: for every dollar of venture capital invested by the venture capital firms, angel investors put up ten. If you can find them.

While the venture capital firms are known to the public—on library reference lists, on the Internet, even in the yellow pages—there is no real resource for finding angel investors. In fact, for obvious reasons, a lot of them don't want to be found—at least, not by just anybody.

If and when the start-up company or early-stage enterprise does find an angel investor, or perhaps when it applies to a venture capital institution, the method of financing that will be used is what is called a private placement.

"Private" is the operative word. In contrast to a public offering, a private-placement sale of securities need not be registered with the government. But you also must limit the people to whom you sell the stock and the way in which you solicit them.

In fact, there can't be anything public about a private placement. You may not advertise a private placement. You may not promote it on a Web site. Instead, you must approach prospective investors one on one. And as I first mentioned in chapter 8, what's more, these people you approach must be accredited investors—individuals who either have a net worth of at least $1 million or have had an annual income of more than $200,000 for the last three years.

In other words, if you know or can get to a fairly large number of significantly affluent people or institutions, you may solicit them, in a private transaction, to invest in your company. When you do solicit them, you are asking them to buy an illiquid stock that will not trade on any market. Indeed, by law the securities that are sold in private placements are restricted from resale for a period of time—generally a year.

Since private-placement investors cannot hope for immediate liquidity, they are betting that the stock will appreciate in value until the company is taken public and they can sell their shares at a profit. Or, alternatively, the company will do well enough to be bought out by a larger company, and the private-placement investors will make their profit in the buyout.

For entrepreneurs seeking backing in the early stages of their enterprise, none of this venture capital or angel investment is easy to come by. It requires work, time, resources, and plenty of agony. Resilience and a thick skin don't hurt, either. You might raise hundreds of thousands of dollars from affluent friends, colleagues, and relatives. But raising millions that way is almost unheard of. By the same token, you might spend great chunks of time and effort applying to venture capital firms, only to find out, months down the road, that the firm has decided not to fund your deal.

I feel that my own experience is instructive. To get seed money for Spring Street, I went to friends, relatives, friends of relatives, and relatives of friends. I managed to raise $800,000—an excellent start, but hardly enough to build a beer empire.

I also approached the venture capital firms. In contrast to the individual investors who had taken a flyer on Wit Beer in the private placements, the firms were fairly easy to find, but their rigorous demands for business plans and projections and analyses, their endless interviewing and discussing, their requests for yet another presentation to yet another set of managers proved numbingly onerous. The process was also extremely time-consuming; in the time it took the venture capital firms to ponder, consider, and decide, we might easily have gone under had we not found other sources of funds.

But Internet venture capital is a whole other ball game, and Internet venture capitalists like Wit Capital offer start-up and early-stage entrepreneurs a whole new opportunity.

Via the Internet, we open the venture capital process to individual retail investors. For emerging enterprises, that means a whole new population of potential providers of venture capital.

First of all, they get the capital without the pressures that typically come from being a publicly traded company. With Internet venture capital, the early-stage company isn't under the eye of analysts whose quarterly projections they have to meet. Too often, meeting those projections means concentrating on short-term goals and objectives that may either deflect the company from long-term strategy or even work to its disadvantage in the critical development stages of a company's life.

Internet venture capital offerings also give issuers control over when to create liquidity for their shares. As long as the offering price represents a fair valuation, prospects for traditional (or digital) IPOs in the future remain bright. Alternatively, if a major IPO does not materialize, the company could still arrange for liquidity through NASDAQ or a stock exchange listing.

Internet venture capital is also a revolutionary opportunity for retail investors, the first time ever that they have had a meaningful chance to invest in start-up and early-stage companies.

Traditionally, if you were a $5,000 investor looking for a long-term equity success, you have had no chance to get in on the ground floor of a risky venture, no matter how willing you might be to take the risk. All you could ever get for your $5,000 was an up-or-down bet on liquid stocks that had already been flipped and traded up in the national markets, stocks that had already returned their best yield. The choice rewards had been seized beforehand by the company issuing stock in an IPO, by the venture capitalists who owned the stock at the time it went public, by the hedge funds and investment bankers taking their cut. Such rewards, however, are exactly what Internet venture capital firms like Wit Capital are offering to the $5,000 investor. To the $2,500 investor. Even to the $1,000 investor. Investors who can be every bit as sophisticated as those with more to spend. Investors who deserve an equal chance to risk what they can afford for the chance at a great reward. Call it public venture capital.

We make it possible because we're using Internet technology to pioneer a new type of offering—an offering that is in essence a hybrid between a digital public offering and a traditional private placement.

As we do with IPOs, for a public venture capital offering, Wit Capital's professional staff will perform such traditional investment banking functions as due diligence and deal structure and valuation. We will work with the company to prepare digital offering documents as well as multimedia audio and visual presentations—the types of materials that would constitute the electronic road show. We will file the deal with the SEC and state Blue Sky regulators so that they are legally salable to the public and not limited to accredited investors.

In contrast to the shares that are typically sold in public offerings, however, the resale of shares offered in public venture capital offerings will be restricted—very much the way shares sold in private placements are restricted.

Of course, before investing in these types of offerings, investors will have to satisfy Wit Capital that speculative investments are suitable for them. This is to some extent a relative inquiry, but Wit Capital takes seriously the need to make it crystal clear that these public venture capital securities are a high-risk investment, that they do not trade on a stock market but rather have resales restricted by the terms of the security, and that it is therefore likely to be some time before they will yield a return.

If ever. It is of course possible that the company will fail completely and the investment will be lost. It is also possible that the company will succeed only modestly, not well enough to go public or be bought out, or even support a thin, liquid market. Then it will be very difficult for the investor to recoup his investment.

But it is also possible that the company will take off and become wildly successful. That's what the investor is betting on—any investor, from the venture capitalist backed by huge institutions to the individual who wants to put a couple of thousand dollars into something he likes or believes in.

The average investment in Spring Street Brewing when we sold its illiquid stock to the public was less than $600. The people investing that amount—thirty-five hundred of them—knew something about beer, about the company, about the industry. Or maybe they just liked our product. But their knowledge and predilection were sufficient that they were willing to back them with hard cash.

In fact, knowledge and predilection are key to the way Wit Capital markets venture capital opportunities. In our view, the most likely backers of any young venture are going to be people who know the product or service or industry, people who have already formed some judgment about the prospects of the company, people who are not simply acting on an uneducated hunch.

If we had a venture capital deal for an outdoor equipment company, for example, we would try to target hikers and backpackers, fishermen and snorkelers, mountain bikers and mountain climbers through all the Web sites that appeal to such people, the kinds of people who would appreciate the particular products our company is developing, the kinds of people with an automatic affinity for the business.

In return, once people have bought their small pieces of the start-up or early-stage company, we will try to educate them about venture capital investing. We will continue to urge them to invest in areas they know something about and to diversify their portfolios.

If an investor comes to us with $50,000, for example, we might advise investing in ten deals of $5,000 each—different deals in different industries. The power of all those small investors adds up. Eventually, I believe, they will wield more clout than all the angel investors and venture capitalists in the world.

It's in the numbers. Need $10 million to make your company grow? Go find ten millionaires. Sell them on the idea of your company, your product, yourself. Or, share the opportunity of your company's future globally over the Internet. Instead of ten millionaires, find two thousand people with $5,000 each. Or five thousand people with $2,000 each. For the high-quality venture capital opportunity— and it's up to Wit Capital to find them, cultivate them, and ensure that they are offered to you at fair prices—the Internet can be the portal to an endless supply of capital.

22.

Private Placements

Notwithstanding the huge benefits available to entrepreneurial companies that tap public venture capital, the highly public nature of the process will not be every issuing company's cup of tea.

The process requires the issuer to comply with public registration requirements, to expose proprietary technical or financial or strategic information to public scrutiny, and to let potential competitors know what you've got in your toolkit. That won't be to the liking of every early-stage company.

Others will perhaps not mind having to disclose information but will balk instead at the expense. Companies seeking relatively small amounts of capital in particular may be unwilling to expend limited resources on the required public filings of the regulatory process.

For those companies guarding their privacy and those husbanding their resources, whether early-stage companies not ready for an IPO or companies with proven track records and headed by experienced management, the private placement may well be the preferred route to venture capital. The problem is that the retail accredited investor has very little access to quality private placements. And unless you belong to a group like the Band of Angels, or have a stockbroker who's willing to pass along word of such deals, your chances of finding private deals are just that: chance.

Most brokerage firms, in fact, have historically had little interest in putting their customers on to private placements. The reason is simple, if selfish: the last thing traditional brokers want is for their customers to put assets in long-term, illiquid investments. Brokers steer customers toward liquid portfolios and frequent trading. When customers trade, after all, brokers get commissions. In most cases, they also keep the spread or receive payment for order flow—none of which is available unless there is trading and liquidity.

While some smaller brokerage firms do specialize in private placements, it is usually on a regional or local market basis, or only for their institutional customers. The result is a highly fragmented private placement market in which the average accredited investor sees only a few good deals a year. What's more, because these firms operate with small networks of investors, the minimum investments set for the private placements tend to be large—as much $50,000 minimum investment. This means that even wealthy investors find it hard to build a diversified portfolio of private-placement investments.

Wit Capital and the Internet are planning to change all that. By serving basically as a clearinghouse for private placements, Wit enables would-be private-placement issuers and investors to simply bypass the brokerage houses. Once again, the Internet becomes the medium that directly matches buyer and seller, investor and issuer.

In eliminating intermediaries, the Wit process also reduces transaction costs, saving issuers money. It offers the investor a much larger selection of private transactions than are typically available from brokers—and with more affordable minimum investment requirements. All of this means, of course, that Wit customers will have an easier time building those all-important diversified portfolios.

Here's how it works:

First, on the issuer side, for any private placement offered, Wit Capital's investment bankers perform the traditional functions of due diligence, valuation determination, deal structure, and memorandum preparation. We assist the issuer in preparing digital offering documents as well as multimedia audio and visual road show presentations. In a typical, paper-based private placement, the offering memorandum is a document an inch thick, and the costs of printing it and mailing it to a thousand people or so can be prohibitive. On the Internet, the offering material is a small packet of kilobytes. The production and mailing costs are nonexistent.

Instead, the offering material, those kilobytes of information artfully and attractively designed, simply go up on our Web site. Not just anywhere, however; we place it in a specially encrypted private-placement area. The encryption limits access to the material to a universe of investors who have been pre-identified as the potential private-placement market.

This is precisely the sort of thing computing technology can do best: it quickly sorts and filters a mass of information, organizing it in various ways. Within our database of prospective investors, we have first organized it to identify those who qualify as accredited investors. Within that identification, we have isolated accredited investors interested in private placements. Only those investors we have pinpointed through these sorts will get access to the private-placements section.

We alert them to the offer by a special E-mail they can open only with their own passwords; the E-mail contains an icon that links the investor instantly to the section of the site containing the private-placement offer. This is not just a cost-effective productivity measure; it is also a highly specific form of targeted marketing.

Once the targeted market has access to the offering material, of course, the usual Wit Capital process takes over: investors directly negotiate and execute the investment transaction, with the usual back-office support from Wit Capital.

Once again, for both issuing company and interested investor, the Internet is providing a whole new way of doing business.

23.

The Digital Stock Market

For most of the last century, the average full-service brokerage firm has earned hundreds of dollars in commission on an average stock trade. Such fees were traditionally seen as appropriate to recompense the firm as a whole for its aggregated experience, expertise, and guidance, as well as for the trade transaction.

Then in the 1970s, a number of so-called discount brokers—Charles Schwab and Fidelity prominent among them—challenged the traditional model of broker commissions. A new model emerged, one that recognized that technology had dramatically reduced the cost of executing a trade. It also recognized that broker advice and expertise might not be as significant or valuable as brokers want investors to believe.

First of all, some of the advice brokers give their customers comes at the behest of the brokers' bosses, who often have their own reasons for promoting a particular stock. Perhaps the firm has underwritten the initial public offering of the shares and has a vested interest in its success, as one example. Or maybe the firm's trading department has taken a long position in a security and now wants to on-load shares.

Second, there is something of an inherent conflict in a traditional broker's advice: how can advice be objective when it is given by a person who gets paid only when he persuades a customer to buy or sell a security? There is little incentive for the broker ever to advise an investor to hold on to an investment for the long term, to build growth in slow, steady increments while avoiding transaction costs and saving on taxes.

Third, in today's world, the timeliness of broker advice is a joke. What makes its usefulness dubious is that, typically, the brokerage house's research department prepares a report and the report is circulated to institutional clients; by the time it gets to retail investors in a phone call from a broker, it is old news. The insight was analyzed long ago. The market has moved. The money has been made. If that's all you're getting from your broker, then you surely should not be paying a high commission for it.

But these were the time-honored traditions, encrusted with age, that discount brokers confronted and overthrew. With technology lowering the cost of the transaction execution and undermining the value of the so-called expertise delivered, the discount brokers aced the former, gave up on the latter, and slashed traditional commissions in half.

Electronic brokers—Wit Capital is one of them—can slash commissions much more. Our process is completely automated. We do not need and do not have any branch offices. No live brokers on the telephone. No receptionist creating a new arrangement of fresh flowers every day. Just a bunch of computers hooked together and a staff of experienced customer service professionals—not a single one of whom is driven by the need to make commissions.

You don't "walk in" to effect a transaction. You log on or pick up your Touch-Tone phone. Your account application is completed online. The data passes directly into our databases without a single stroke of human labor or intervention.

At the click of a button, you get easy and immediate access to up-to-the-second information and analysis—world news, business headlines, stock quotes. You can even request to be alerted when there is new market data or company-specific information available.

When you want to trade, your trade is ordered on-line or via Touch-Tone telephone. And it is executed on-line, routed directly to a marketplace in a matter of seconds.

You also have complete access to your entire portfolio—on-line, in real time, twenty-four hours a day.

Click for date of purchase, cost basis, current price, market value. It's all there, up to the minute.

Click for account information: detailed balance and transaction data, buying power, net market portfolio value, dividends paid, interest earned, deposits and withdrawals.

Yet all this—the lowered cost and expanded content of the service—is just the tip of the iceberg. The real treasure at the heart of this financial future is Wit Capital's digital stock market. In the digital stock market, you not only save the commission, you save the spread.

Remember how the big institutions trade stock? They don't call a broker who then calls a specialist or market maker. They just boot up their desktops and check the order book on the computer screen. Then they click their mouses to play hit-or-take or the auction market.

No dealer, no market-making middleman, no spread, no payment for order flow. The trade is executed directly between buyer and seller, and the electronic trading facility that has made all of this possible takes its tiny fee per share traded.

Until recently, however, it was inconceivable that a similar mechanism could provide similar benefits to individual retail investors. You couldn't just attach retail investors' PCs to Instinet or Posit because the costs for leased lines and interface connections alone would have been prohibitive.

Enter the Internet, a low-cost, public network that rendered leased lines and interface connections a moot point. Enter then Wit Capital, making use of the Internet to allow investors to participate in a direct matching trade. In fact, our Global Trade system makes retail investors their own broker-dealers. It gives them the capability to create and execute just about any type of trade transaction. That's going to change the investment industry altogether.

For limit orders, where a buyer won't buy above a certain price and a seller won't sell below it, we have created two types of trading executions. The first is a simple hit-or-take execution. An electronic order book contains validated buy or sell orders ranked by price and the time of the order. The investor scrolls up or down the screen and hits a buy or takes a sell by clicking on the pertinent order. Obviously, since no market makers are involved, investors will get a better price from our electronic order book than they would if they were executing orders through a broker in one of the national marketplaces.

The second type of execution is a negotiated one. Suppose, for example, an investor wants to sell 1,000 shares of stock at $100 per share. Browsing the order book one day, he sees a buy order for 1,000 shares at $99 per share. That's not exactly where he wants to trade, but it's close. It is at least the start of a conversation, so the seller taps a couple of clicks on the keyboard and arranges to go into a chat room with the buyer.

This is not an E-mail negotiation (although, of course, such a thing is possible); rather, it's an on-line interactive "conversation" in which buyer and seller type in alternating statements and responses. "You want to buy 1,000 shares of ABC Corporation?" the seller might type.

"Right," comes back the message from the buyer.

"I'm selling at $100," says the seller. "Take it?"

"No," counters the buyer. "I want to pay $99."

Counter-counter-offer from the seller: "Split the difference at $99.50?"

"Sold," says the buyer.

Once buyer and seller agree, the system routes the trade to a clearing and settlement firm that completes the execution. The clearing firm also ensures that no party is exposed to credit risk.

The system also accepts undisclosed orders. An investor might put in a sell order for 1,000 shares at a particular ask price, but he would mark the order with a special code. The order book would simply report that somebody wanted to sell shares in a particular stock. Neither the number of shares nor the ask price would be indicated, although, of course, the complete information would be lodged within the computer. It could then identify a match from among the buy orders on the other side of the book.

The advantage for the investor in not fully exposing his position is a strategic one. If a buyer knows exactly how much stock the investor is selling, and at exactly what price, the buying strategy might shift, and that, in turn, could actually move the market. An undisclosed order, however, shows only an interest in selling stock. There's no particular strategic advantage to either buyer or seller; there's just an automatic matching and a cleanly executed trade.

Wit Capital's Global Trade system is also a mechanism for price improvement on market orders—that is, orders to buy or sell that are to be executed at the best possible price and as soon as possible. We will do it by creating what is essentially a national auction for retail orders. Most Internet users are aware of the many auction sites on the Net today, enabling consumers to offer or bid for everything from wine to real estate, cars to computers. Our auction works on the same general principles.

We will take an order—say, to sell stock in ABC Corporation—and we will broadcast it over the Internet through a special proprietary interface we have developed. This activates a pop-up screen on the computers of all the people following the auction. It's an audience that will include such professionals as computer model traders and options specialists, as well as retail investors looking to put some liquidity into the market.

The screen shows a clock that counts down the time available for putting in a bid. Within that time limit, anybody watching must decide whether to trade against the order, what price to bid, and how to state the bid—whether in quarters or eighths or sixteenths or thirty-seconds.

Investors can actually preprogram their computers to stay tuned to all auctions in a particular stock. That way, they can strategize building or reducing an inventory. Alternatively, they can just put up a market order to sell, then wait for the auction to surface the best bid price.

When the clock has counted down to the end of the bidding period, the computer crunches all the bids in an algorithm, and whoever has bid the best price gets the trade.

Instead of a market controlled by dealers, the Internet auction will be open to all. Instead of the market makers controlling order flow, the order will go to whoever gives the best price.

All of these trading options—for limit and market orders, for undisclosed orders and negotiated deals and auction pricing—offer a new level of stock-trading efficiency that should bring real benefits to individual investors—specifically, better prices when they trade NASDAQ and listed shares.

If that rattles the cushioned cocoon of complacency in which broker-dealers now thrive and sends them back into the fray of customer-driven market forces, so be it. Perhaps it will propel them back to their first obligation: serving their customers' best interests. And that, in turn, may stir the competitive and creative juices of all the participants in the stock-trading process.

This is no small mission—and it's not going to happen all at once.

At first, in fact, Wit Capital will limit trading in the digital stock market to a selection of high-quality NASDAQ stocks that have strong prospects but still trade at wide spreads. The new marketplace can effect significant savings on these spreads, and that should attract yet more buyers and sellers.

Initially, also, in order to comply with current regulations on electronic trading systems, trading will be limited to executions that occur within the spreads of the NASDAQ market.

This is also important for our investors; it would serve no one if an investor somehow got caught in technology's blind spot and wound up with a worse trade than could have been gotten from a traditional broker.

Ultimately, however, Wit Capital's digital stock market will expand in a number of directions. It will add more and more securities, well beyond the initial NASDAQ stocks. As volume grows, it will move to the forefront, becoming the market for certain securities.

Of course, that conclusion awaits the overcoming of not inconsiderable technological and regulatory challenges. And it will require a major marketing and educational effort vis-à-vis a public that, if not skeptical, is for the most part unaware of developments in and the potential of the digital stock market.

Fortunately, however, in all three of these areas—technology, regulation, and public awareness—the trends are favorable.

Technological advances are knocking down barriers to the digital stock market with every passing day. New versions of encryption and fire-wall technologies put pay to the lingering doubts about the security of electronic trading systems. This is obviously essential. If investors do not feel secure with digital trading, they will not trade. As of today, they can feel absolutely secure.

Technology's onward-and-upward momentum is also making for real-time price updates a matter of course. Thanks to Java, the new language from Sun Microsystems, this feature can now be accommodated on a screen-based trading system. It means that the investor who is on-line can actually get up and go get a cup of coffee, knowing that when he gets back to his screen, he'll be looking at current, up-to-the-minute price quotes.

He might also be looking at a late-breaking announcement that has been multicast to him and to thousands of other investors simultaneously. New multicasting technology is moving the World Wide Web beyond being a very large fax machine, sending lots of messages one at a time, to becoming a huge broadcast television that sends a single message simultaneously to everyone who is tuned in.

As technology proceeds apace, the regulatory environment is also changing—at long last. Nudged by the likes of Instinet, POSIT, and AZX, and, frankly, shoved ahead hard by the Wit-Trade phenomenon, the SEC of Commissioner Wallman and his colleagues has made a concerted effort to unfreeze the regulatory climate. Step by step, Wallman et al. have not just accommodated but have actually encouraged the entrepreneurial application of technologies to spur competition within and among stock markets.

In the spring of 1997, in fact, the SEC published a concept release seeking comments on a proposal to streamline the regulatory framework for a digital stock market. That may be a personal triumph for Wit Capital; it is also a wake-up call for traditional stock markets.

The traditional stock markets should also pay closer attention to what is happening in public opinion, the third trend proving favorable to our digital stock market. It is certainly fair to say that most people know very little about how stocks trade. They understand even less about the complexities of marketplaces, spreads, and payments for order flow. It is also fair to say that this ignorance is no accident. The brokerage industry has never been interested in letting the light shine in on their operations. Its powerful lobbying apparat, the National Association of Securities Dealers, has enjoyed a fairly cozy relationship with both members of Congress and staffers of the various regulatory agencies. If there has not exactly been collusion to keep the lid on how stocks trade and stock markets work, there has certainly been no desire to raise the lid.

But as always happens, the broker-dealer community grew complacent. Its overreaching reached too far. In recent years, the SEC has stepped in quickly and forcefully, instigating a number of high-profile investigations into the practices of market makers and the ways that spreads have been artificially maintained.

A large television audience was watching when a group of New York dealers were caught on tape colluding to keep a competitor from offering a narrower spread.

A large newspaper readership saw the headlines when Congress threatened to impose legislation requiring that stock prices be quoted in decimals, not fractions. No more innocent-looking traditions to mask unfair practices, Congressmen railed, as the major exchanges voluntarily agreed to use decimals.

What the public heard in these and other front-page stories was the rusty creaking of an old-fashioned system, a system in which ordinary retail investors had little part; a remote, aloof system that suddenly seemed as out-of-date as the bewigged brokers under the buttonwood tree two centuries ago.

And what the public is just beginning to sense is what I believe: in the future, the stock market will not revolve around brokers or dealers or specialists. It will not be limited to a physical location, to a trading floor, even to a single central database. The stock market of the future will take place whenever individuals access each other to trade securities. A seat on tomorrow's stock exchange is any chair in front of a computer with a modem.

24.

It's a Community, Stupid!

We hear it all the time:

The Internet is just so much overhyping. The World Wide Web is just a worldwide wait. The Internet? It's where GIGO reigns. GIGO, for Garbage In, Garbage Out. The Web is never going to amount to much or change anybody's life for the better.

The people who mouth these clichés in my view couldn't be more wrong. I think they haven't the slightest idea as to what's going on here, and what the future holds. In fact, I think the Internet is under-hyped and that its true significance is only now beginning to be understood.

Yes, it connects vendors with customers—free of charge. Publishers with readers. Brokers with investors.

Yes, all of that cuts costs. The costs of shipping documents, printing catalogues, publishing newspapers.

Yes, it cuts out the middleman, saving his salary and overhead and office rental and sales staff and markup, yielding additional savings. Buy your book at Amazon.com. Order your airline tickets on-line. Trade your stocks by clicking on icons. You've disintermediated the intermediary; you deserve to pocket a few bucks.

But basically, all of that just amounts to running a straighter line between two points. It's faster and it's cheaper. But it's hardly what the futurists call a paradigm shift.

That will come, I believe, not just from the Web's efficiencies and cost-saving convenience, but from the communities it enables. Community, in my view, is the real transforming power of the Net. It's the true "killer app." It creates something not just faster, cheaper, and better, but something altogether different, a new kind of activity that comes from the connections among individuals.

The great entrepreneurial opportunity of the Web is to facilitate these Web communities.

That is what we're doing at Wit Capital. We're a brokerage firm, yes, but so is E-Trade or e.Schwab, providing very, very low commissions. The transforming value of our operation will only become entirely evident when the Wit community organizes around Wit activities. A sustained community of sophisticated investors interacting with one another: it offers the potential for awesome change.

In the digital stock market, for example, where investors will interact to post orders and negotiate trades, value will come to each member from other members. Together, they gain something they could not find anywhere else.

In investment banking, member interaction can position Wit Capital to win access to high-quality transactions or, alternatively, demonstrate that the transaction is not that high-quality after all. Suppose our Wit community evidences strong interest in a biotechnology issue. That becomes a ready-made shareholder base—a source of capital—that is instantly very attractive to the issuer. That gives the community leverage.

Sufficient leverage, for example, to induce issuers to present their wares directly to the Wit community, thus eliciting an instant reaction, as members either place orders or move to the next offering. Isn't this the primary securities market as it was meant to be?

For those investors wary of advice from brokers in business to peddle stocks, what about an open bulletin board where the community can share experiences, insights, opinions?

But that's just the beginning. In time, the community itself becomes, for Wit Capital, a new source of revenue. Access to the community becomes a desideratum we can market—under strict rules that protect privacy. An insurance company wants to reach you? A mutual fund? A travel services firm? Sign a pledge of nonintrusiveness and we'll negotiate. And members of the community will vote with their wallets for the types of goods and services they want to buy through Wit Capital.

Over time, these additional revenue sources will enable Wit Capital consistently to lower the costs of our trading and brokerage services. Eventually, the services might become loss leaders operated for the good of the community, mechanisms that simply bring in more and more investors, because a bigger community means more capacity for Wit Capital to underwrite stocks and provide more liquidity in the stock market. Until finally the Wit Capital community is treated to commission-free trading. It's a powerful point, and it's a momentous threat to the old-fashioned business establishment that does not understand what on-line communities are all about.

Right now, for example, the large, full-service brokerage firms spend most of their time worrying about deep-discount brokers on the Internet stealing their customers with commissions of $14.99. They haven't yet given a thought to the kind of investor community I've just described, a community with so many members, with revenue from so many varied sources, that it can give away brokerage services for free, earning its daily bread by underwriting stocks or selling advertising or tax preparation services or all of the above.

How will the traditional brokerages compete when they face firms that provide all the core services brokers now provide but require none of their traditional revenue streams?

I'm betting that the answer is: they won't.

I invite you to join the Wit Capital community. We're located at witcapital.com on the Internet. Why not have a seat, boot up, and log on? Open a beer. Take a sip. Be patient: it won't all arrive in a day. But I think you'll enjoy the ride.

Epilogue
Wit's End: Just the Beginning

On September 23, 1997, Wit Capital Corporation made financial history when it became the first Internet investment bank to participate in a major underwritten public offering, digitally distributing shares of C. H. Robinson Worldwide's common stock to individual investors on a first-come, first-served basis. The deal was lead-managed by B. T. Alex Brown.

Three weeks later, Wit Capital made history again, commencing the first-ever public venture capital offering for Sandbox Entertainment, a three-year-old developer of Internet game software.

Meanwhile, Spring Street Brewing Company has swelled the ranks of its staff to a total of seven people in 1997. The company's fourth product, a lemon grass and mint-spiced wheat beer, is scheduled for launch in the first quarter of 1998.

Construction proceeds apace on the company's first brewing facility—a fifteen-barrel open-fermenting Belgian brewhouse in downtown Manhattan's legendary meatpacking district. Plans were drawn up for a Belgian-style brasserie-café within the brewery. The menu will feature mussels and French fries, and, of course, cold beer brewed on the premises.

The idea is to call the brewery and café, simply, Wit.

Index